THE BIRTH OF JESUS

THE BIRTH OF JESUS

Biblical and Theological Reflections

Edited by
GEORGE J. BROOKE

T&T CLARK
EDINBURGH

T&T CLARK LTD
59 GEORGE STREET
EDINBURGH EH2 2LQ
SCOTLAND
www.tandtclark.co.uk

First published 2000

ISBN 0 567 08756 5

British Library Cataloguing-in-Publication Data
A catalogue record for this book is available from the British Library

Typeset by Waverley Typesetters, Galashiels
Printed and bound in Great Britain by MPG Books, Bodmin

To the memory of
Anthony O. Dyson
1935–1998

Samuel Ferguson Professor of Social and Pastoral Theology
University of Manchester
1980–1998

Professor Emeritus
1998

CONTENTS

ACKNOWLEDGEMENTS

Permission to include a substantial extract from a published work is gratefully acknowledged as follows: from HarperCollins for the quotation from *The First Messiah: Investigating the Savior Before Christ* by Michael Wise (New York: HarperCollins Publishers Inc., 1999). Many of the brief scriptural quotations contained herein are from the *New Revised Standard Version of the Bible*, copyrighted 1989, by the Division of Christian Education of the National Council of the Churches of Christ in the United States of America and are used by permission (all rights reserved). Permission from the Librarian of the John Rylands University Library of Manchester to reproduce Rylands Ivory Plaque Number 6 on the front cover is also gratefully acknowledged.

CONTRIBUTORS

PHILIP S. ALEXANDER is Professor of Post-Biblical Jewish Literature in the Department of Religions and Theology at the University of Manchester. From 1992–5 he was President of the Oxford Centre for Hebrew and Jewish Studies. Amongst his many publications are *Textual Sources for the Study of Judaism* (Manchester: Manchester University Press, 1984) and, with G. Vermes, *Qumran Cave 4.XIX: Serekh ha-Yahad and Two Related Texts* (Oxford: Clarendon Press, 1998).

GEORGE J. BROOKE has taught at the University of Manchester since 1984. Since 1998 he has been Rylands Professor of Biblical Criticism and Exegesis in the Department of Religions and Theology. He has authored many studies on the Dead Sea Scrolls including *Exegesis at Qumran: 4QFlorilegium in its Jewish Context* (Sheffield: JSOT Press, 1985) and *The Allegro Qumran Collection* (Leiden: Brill, 1996). He has edited or co-edited and contributed to *Temple Scroll Studies* (Sheffield: JSOT Press, 1989), *Septuagint, Scrolls and Cognate Studies* (Atlanta: Scholars Press, 1992), *Women in the Biblical Tradition* (Lewiston: Edwin Mellen Press, 1992), *New Qumran Texts and Studies* (Leiden: Brill, 1994), *Narrativity in Biblical and Related Texts* (Leuven: Peeters, 2000), and *Jewish Ways of Reading the Bible* (Oxford: Oxford University Press, 2000).

F. GERALD DOWNING is an Honorary Research Fellow in the Centre for Biblical Studies in the Department of Religions and

Theology in the University of Manchester. From 1990–7 he was vicar of Bolton and before that Vice-Principal of the Northern Ordination Course in Manchester. He has published widely on both biblical and theological topics. His books include *Jesus and the Threat of Freedom* (London: SCM Press, 1987), *Christ and the Cynics* (Sheffield: Sheffield Academic Press, 1988), *Cynics and Christian Origins* (Edinburgh: T&T Clark, 1992), *Cynics, Paul and the Pauline Churches* (London: Routledge, 1998), *Making Sense in (and of) the First Christian Century* and *Doing Things with Words in the First Christian Century* (both Sheffield: Sheffield Academic Press, 2000).

ELAINE GRAHAM is Samuel Ferguson Professor of Social and Pastoral Theology in the Department of Religions and Theology at the University of Manchester. Her publications include *Making the Difference: Gender, Personhood and Theology* (London: Mowbray, 1995) and *Transforming Practice: Pastoral Theology in an Age of Uncertainty* (London: Mowbray, 1996); she has also edited or co-edited *Windows and Walls: A Housing Action Handbook for Churches* (Manchester: Church Action on Poverty, 1991) and *Life Cycles: Women and Pastoral Care* (London: SPCK, 1993).

GRACE M. JANTZEN is Research Professor in Religion, Culture and Gender in the Department of Religions and Theology at the University of Manchester. Her publications include *God's World, God's Body* (London: Darton, Longman & Todd, 1984), *Julian of Norwich: Mystic and Theologian* (London: SPCK, 1987; second edition 2000), *Power, Gender and Christian Mysticism* (Cambridge: Cambridge University Press, 1995), and *Becoming Divine: Towards a Feminist Philosophy of Religion* (Manchester: Manchester University Press, 1998).

TODD KLUTZ is Lecturer in New Testament Studies in the Department of Religions and Theology at the University of Manchester. He has written *With Authority and Power: Exorcism as Social Discourse in Luke–Acts* (Cambridge: Cambridge University Press, forthcoming) and has been commissioned to write the study guide on *The Testament of Solomon* for Sheffield Academic Press.

R. BARRY MATLOCK has been Lecturer in New Testament Studies in the Department of Biblical Studies at the University of Sheffield since 1994. He is Director of the Department's Centre for Bible, Theology and Praxis. A specialist in Pauline Studies, he has written *Unveiling the Apocalyptic Paul: Paul's Interpreters and the Rhetoric of Criticism* (Sheffield: Sheffield Academic Press, 1996).

ARTHUR PEACOCKE was Director of the Ian Ramsey Centre in the Faculty of Theology at the University of Oxford from 1984–8 and from 1995–9. Before moving to a career engaging directly in the interface between theology and the natural sciences, he taught and researched in the field of physical biochemistry. His publications include *Science and the Christian Experiment* (London: Oxford University Press, 1971), *Creation and the World of Science* (Oxford: Clarendon Press, 1979), *Intimations of Reality* (Notre Dame: University of Notre Dame Press, 1984), *God and the New Biology* (London: Dent, 1986), *Theology for a Scientific Age* (London: SCM Press, 1993), *From DNA to Dean* (Norwich: The Canterbury Press, 1996), and *God and Science: A Quest for Christian Credibility* (London: SCM Press, 1996).

GRAHAM WARD is Professor of Contextual Theology and Ethics in the Department of Religions and Theology at the University of Manchester. Before coming to Manchester in 1998 he was Dean of Peterhouse in Cambridge. His publications include *Barth, Derrida and the Language of Theology* (Cambridge: Cambridge University Press, 1995), *Theology and Contemporary Critical Theory* (Basingstoke: Macmillan, 1996), *The Postmodern God: A Theological Reader* (Oxford: Blackwell, 1997) and *The Certeau Reader* (Oxford: Blackwell, 2000).

INTRODUCTION

George J. Brooke

The movement of the world's chronometer from 1999 to 2000 caused the largest display of fireworks the world has ever known. Purists argue that the dawn of the new millennium has been celebrated a year early, since 2000 is properly the last year of the second millennium rather than the first year of the third. Nobody can deny, however, the way in which vast numbers of people have seen some significance in the change of date. Most of these people are not practising Christians and so have not been explicitly celebrating the supposed arrival of the two thousandth year since the birth of Jesus, as the revisions to the fifth-century work of Dionysius Exiguus encourage many to suppose.

Academic theologians have not been immune to this marking of the passing of time. Since the system of dating does indeed have something to do with Jesus, in Manchester we thought it suitable to mark the year 2000 by having a symposium around the theme of the birth of Jesus. Together with two guests, Barry Matlock from Sheffield and Arthur Peacocke from Oxford, seven of us from the Department of Religions and Theology at the University of Manchester put together a programme for a day's conference which would be open to anybody from the local community who might wish to attend. The purpose of the day was to address the topic of the birth of Jesus from our own specialist concerns in Biblical Studies, Gender Studies, Jewish Studies,

Pastoral Theology, Philosophy of Religion, Science and Religion, and Theology. We did not set out to provide any elaborate exegetical interpretation of the birth and infancy narratives in the Gospels, though several of the contributions interact with those Gospel passages. What emerged was a remarkably fresh and enjoyable collection of presentations which it seemed to us would be worthwhile to offer to a wider public as a short book. We have attempted to retain the freshness of the original presentations, so in most cases notes have been kept to a minimum and placed at the end of the book.

The picture on the front cover of this book captures much of the mood of this set of essays. It has an obvious Manchester connection as it is a photograph of an ivory plaque in the John Rylands University Library of Manchester (Rylands Ivory Plaque No. 6). Considered to be from the sixth century AD its precise provenance is unknown. It came into the collection of Manchester's Rylands library when the library acquired the immensely valuable Crawford collection of manuscripts and printed books. The plaque has four holes in it which indicate that it must at one time have been pinned to something. It also has bevelled edges, showing that it was inset in some way. It has been suggested that it may have been part of a highly ornamented front cover for a Gospel book, but there is no certainty of that.

The plaque delightfully complements the concerns of this collection of essays in several ways. To begin with it shows that one picture is never enough for capturing the significance of the birth of Jesus. The upper panel is a depiction of the infant Jesus receiving the wise men and their gifts, a traditional reflection of the epiphany as reflected in Matthew's Gospel. In the lower panel the infant Jesus is no longer in the centre but to one side in a solidly constructed manger surrounded by the animals of Isaiah 1.3 ('The ox knows its owner, and the donkey its master's crib'); the separation of Jesus from his mother is clear and painful, just as it is in Luke's Gospel, even in the simple comment, only in Luke, that Mary wrapped Jesus in bands of cloth and laid him in a manger. One picture is never enough; telling and retelling the birth of Jesus requires and evokes a narrative dynamism.

In addition to asserting that more than one picture is needed, the plaque is rich in symbolism. Part of the richness of the symbolism derives from the carver's attention to the details of the two Gospel accounts. In the upper panel the central focus on the enthroned Jesus echoes Matthew's concern with the way in which Jesus represents the kingship of God. In the lower panel Luke's interest in the place of Jesus in providing meaning to all that was taking place in the Temple is evident. The manger is both crib and brick altar. Jesus is offered as a sacrifice to fulfil all that the sacrificial system was intended for.

The plaque also neatly indicates that what is subsequently confirmed as canonical never seems to be quite enough for carrying all that needs to be said in each new generation about the birth of Jesus. Most obviously the lower panel depicts the story of Salome, the mother of James and John (Matt. 27.56; Mark 15.40), the earliest written form of which is contained in the *Protevangelium of James*. The *Protevangelium of James* probably dates in its written form from no earlier than the middle of the second century AD, since it is clearly dependent on the infancy narratives of Matthew and Luke. In the *Protevangelium of James* 19–20 the story runs as follows. When she leaves the cave where she has witnessed the birth of Jesus, the midwife whom Joseph has sought out meets Salome and speaks of how Mary's virginity has remained intact. In words reminiscent of doubting Thomas, Salome refuses to believe the midwife's claim, unless she physically tests Mary's condition for herself. On making the test, Salome's hand withers away, as if consumed by fire. After she has prayed fervently for her hand's restoration, an angel appears to her and commands her to touch the infant Jesus so that she may be healed. After the miraculous restoration of her hand, Salome is commanded not to reveal what she has seen until Jesus arrives in Jerusalem. The ivory plaque depicts Salome at the moment when her withered hand is restored. To those who see the plaque, the story of Salome's withered hand acts both as a challenge to any who would doubt

Mary's virginity and also as a further attestation of prayer answered and healing received.

Overall, in its attention to the Old Testament the plaque recalls the Jewishness of Jesus and the way in which his birth was understood by many early Christians as the fulfilment of much Jewish expectation. In its twofold representation of Jesus as enthroned and laid on the altar, the plaque stresses that sovereignty demands human sacrifice and kingship is to be seen in human self-offering. The smallness of the Jesus enthroned on his mother's lap and the isolation of Jesus on his crib-altar stress the fragile humanity of the one through whom Christians claim God is revealed. In having two panels with much action in each, the plaque emphasises that the birth of Jesus has a narrative power which appeals and challenges, attracts and provokes. In all this the plaque remains a material artwork which is a multivalent symbolic representation of the meeting of two worlds.

The ivory plaque is thus full of the suggestiveness of the birth of Jesus with which the contributions to this volume are concerned. Some of them consider various aspects of the Jewishness of Jesus. In addition to the obvious echoes of the Hebrew scriptures, the Dead Sea Scrolls, as I suggest, confirm that in the Gospel infancy narratives more features than is commonly supposed have a contemporary background in Jewish traditions. However, the Jewishness of Jesus has not been handled straightforwardly by either Jews or Christians, so the matter remains an ever-relevant topic for examination, as is evident in the contributions by Philip Alexander and Graham Ward. Attention to the Jewishness of Jesus naturally engages with his full humanity and that is discussed further from very different angles in two of the essays here: Barry Matlock expounds clearly what we might suppose Paul made of the fact of Jesus' birth and Arthur Peacocke urges the reader to take full account of contemporary understandings of human biochemistry. The ongoing appeal of the stories of the birth and infancy of Jesus rests also in their very narrativity: Todd Klutz throws new light on the place of virginity in Luke's version of the story and Elaine Graham outlines the interplay between vernacular religion and narrative theology in the contemporary re-enactment of the birth of Jesus in hundreds of places every year. In all this the fact of Jesus' birth remains symbolic, whether in an iconic way as Gerald Downing tentatively suggests in helping us understand a little more about things divine, or as a statement of that hope which Grace Jantzen proposes best expresses the meaning of things human in what it is to be born.

We are grateful to the Small Grants Fund of the Research and Graduate Support Unit of the University of Manchester for financial support which enabled us to set up the day and invite two speakers from outside Manchester. Allen Hall, one of the university's halls of residence, provided the venue for the day and excellent hospitality which was much appreciated by all fifty participants. We are also very grateful to the staff of T&T Clark, especially Dr Geoffrey Green, for accepting this collection of essays for publication and for the swiftness with which the final product has been produced.

This small book is affectionately and respectfully dedicated to the memory of Professor Tony Dyson, a former colleague, friend and teacher in the Department of Religions and Theology at the University of Manchester. We hope the book carries forward his incisive yet open-ended approach to theology in general and to the figure of Jesus in particular. We also hope that readers will enjoy the differing perspectives of this collection and discover new ways of thinking about how the significance of the birth of Jesus can be understood and appropriated in the third millennium.

I

JESUS: FULLY JEWISH AND MORE

CHAPTER ONE

YESHU/YESHUA BEN YOSEF OF NAZARETH: DISCERNING THE JEWISH FACE OF JESUS

Philip S. Alexander

The face of Jesus in art

Why is Jesus so seldom depicted in western Christian art as recognisably Jewish? At first sight the answer seems obvious: till the nineteenth century artists were simply not interested in historical realism. They were content to paint Jesus in the clothes and settings of their own days. This, however, can hardly be the whole story, for Jews are, in fact, from time to time clearly depicted in scenes from Jesus' life, usually in brutal, stereotypical fashion, with hooked noses and Jewish hats, and always as evil, as Christ's enemies or tormentors. The juxtaposition of these Jewish types with Jesus is stark: imagine the effect of reversing the image and showing Jesus with a hooked nose and his tormentors with 'western' features! Hardly anywhere in Christian art can one find even a flicker of recognition that Jesus too was Jewish. His ethnicity is almost totally ignored.

A few pre-nineteenth-century painters do seem to have made a conscious effort to portray a Jewish Jesus. Rembrandt is a case in point. He produced a series of heads of Christ,[1] which are widely recognised as based on a living Jewish type (to my eye they are all modelled on the same face). There is probably no mystery as to how Rembrandt achieved this Jewishness. He lived in Amsterdam on the edge of the Jewish quarter and he loved to go round the corner from his house to the flea market, and observe

9

the picturesque figures, who frequented the place. Some of these were Jewish. He sketched them and used their faces for his faces of Christ. It is interesting that he seems to have been attracted by the rather gaunt, ascetic features of the poorer Ashkenazi Jews who were beginning to move into Amsterdam in the seventeenth century in search of a better life, rather than to the sleek, well-fed faces of the more prosperous Sefardi Jews. It is, perhaps, indicative of Rembrandt's deep compassion and humanity that he should have seen in the faces of the poor Jews in the flea market the face of Jesus. But Rembrandt is something of an exception that proves the rule: western religious artists generally make no effort to represent the Jewishness of Jesus.

It is not that Christianity denied the Jewishness of Jesus. That was always implicitly recognised. It was only with the rise of racist anti-Semitism at the end of the nineteenth century that the claim that Jesus was Aryan was first advanced. One of the leading exponents of this bizarre idea was Houston Stewart Chamberlain. Chamberlain, though English by birth and education, spent most of his life in Germany. He married Richard Wagner's daughter and was a leading figure in Wagner's circle at Bayreuth. Like Wagner he was profoundly anti-Semitic and his magnum opus, *The Foundations of the Nineteenth Century*,[2] which he dedicated, apparently without irony, to one of his former Jewish professors at the University of Vienna, was one of the most influential works of modern racist anti-Semitism. It was in this that he argued that Jesus was, in fact, Aryan. The theory of the Aryan Jesus had a brief vogue in the 1920s and 1930s in Germany, as the Nazis rose to power, but it has always been rejected by the majority of responsible scholars as a total aberration, without a shred of support in historical fact. Mainline Christianity has always implicitly or explicitly acknowledged the Jewishness of Jesus. This makes it all the more puzzling why Christian art has not attempted to depict Jesus as a Jew. Why in an act of collective amnesia or denial has it simply ignored his ethnicity?

Pursuing this line of thinking two further questions come to mind. The first is: What effect would it have had on viewers to have painted a recognisably Jewish Jesus? The impact might well have been profound. It might have stopped them in their tracks with a sense of shock. It would have been comparable to painting Jesus as black with African features, or as Chinese with a Chinese face. What message would such a portrait have conveyed? Most people can recall the powerful image of Che Guevara as Christ. But what message does this convey? Che Guevara as the martyr of a noble revolutionary cause? The Marxist revolutionary as the true saviour of humanity? And what happens when, as some Christian publicists did recently, the image is reappropriated and Jesus shown as Che Guevara? What now is the message? Jesus as the true revolutionary? Such powerful icons are always ambiguous and the way we read them will always be conditioned by our cultural and personal circumstances.

The second question which comes to mind is: How would we paint the Jewishness of Jesus? What features would we give him, and how could we be sure that those features were authentic? Who would have the authority to validate them as authentic and write beneath them, like someone endorsing a passport photograph, 'I hereby certify that this is the true Jewish likeness of Jesus?'

The Jewish Jesus of history

I would like to use these observations on the problems of painting a Jewish Jesus to help us analyse one aspect of the quest for the historical Jesus. Over the past hundred years or so – ever since the rise of modern historical scholarship – there have been numerous attempts to recover the Jesus of history. The quest has gone through various phases, oscillating between optimism that the historical Jesus can be found and pessimism that he can ever be disentangled from the Christ of faith. One aspect of this quest has been precisely the issue of the Jewishness of Jesus. The reasoning has gone something like this. We all acknowledge that Jesus was Jewish. Is not therefore a *Jewish* portrait of Jesus likely to be historically more accurate than one that is not? There are a number of lives of Jesus extant which implicitly claim to be historically accurate at least in part on the grounds that they offer a genuine *Jewish* Jesus. What are we to make of these claims? How credible are they? Let us consider briefly the Jewishness of some Jewish portraits of Jesus.

The Toledot Yeshu

First a traditional Jewish portrait, the so-called *Toledot Yeshu* (the Story of Jesus)[3] which pays particular attention to the details surrounding Jesus' conception and birth. According to one of the common versions of this tale, Yohanan, a learned and pious Jew of the house of David, married a respectable but poor virgin named Miriam. Miriam was raped by a neighbour, a handsome rogue called Joseph Pandera, who tricked her into having intercourse with him by passing himself off as Yohanan her husband. When Miriam became pregnant, Yohanan knew that the child was not his and so abandoned her. Mary called the child Yehoshua after her uncle, but the name was corrupted to Yeshu. Yeshu proved to be bright but wilful and disrespectful of the Sages. When he grew up he dabbled in magic and performed all sorts of miracles by using the ineffable name of God. Finally to stop him leading the people astray the Jewish authorities had to put him to death.

Christians have, not surprisingly, found the *Toledot Yeshu* deeply offensive and it was a prime target for Christian censors. However, it is actually susceptible of more positive readings than is sometimes supposed. The predominant image of Jesus that it conveys is of a rather tragic figure, a potentially good person, of notable family, brought down by a fatal character flaw. The *Toledot Yeshu* exists in around a dozen versions, some of which (probably the later ones) are more offensive than others, though none quite sinks to the level of scurrility of some pagan anti-Christian texts. Though none of the versions in its present form can be earlier than the tenth century at the earliest, certain elements of the story undoubtedly go back to late antiquity (they are found already in the Talmud), and it is not impossible that some preserve genuine first-century traditions.[4] The charge that Jesus was a magician who performed miracles and healings by using dark powers, is found already in the Gospels. We have, then, here a Jewish portrait of Jesus – a picture of how he appeared to those who did not accept his claims or the image of him created by his followers.

The Letter to the Hebrews

The second Jewish portrait of Jesus which I would like to consider comes from the New Testament. Now the objection might be raised that what the New Testament offers is surely a Christian view or views of Jesus, so let me explain. The New Testament, so far as we know, was all written by Jews (and probably for Jews) at a time when the Christian movement had not yet clearly separated from Judaism. All the New Testament writers are eager to portray Jesus as standing within Jewish tradition and as fulfilling the prophecies given to ancient Israel. Some of the New Testament writers begin this process of linking Jesus to prophecy with his conception and birth, others with later events in his life. Whatever the starting point, there is a clear case for taking all New Testament portraits of Jesus as at least *prima facie* Jewish.

The particular New Testament portrait on which I would like briefly to focus is found in the Epistle to the Hebrews. We do not know who wrote Hebrews (it is now generally accepted that it was not Paul), nor to whom it was written (it has been conjectured that its recipients might have been the Qumran community), but it is undoubtedly a sophisticated meditation on the person and work of Jesus. Jesus is represented as the full and final revelation of God in history, the fulfilment of the fragmentary prophecies of the old dispensation. By his death he made atonement for humanity, entering into the heavenly Temple as the true celestial high priest to offer up his sacrifice to God on the heavenly altar. Though in his humanity Jesus was briefly made lower than the angels (Heb. 2.9), the author introduces Jesus without any reference to his human birth and without mentioning his human name. This figure of fulfilment is God's son, appointed heir of all things through whom God created the world. He is the effulgence of God's glory, the very image of the substance of God, and he upholds all things by the word of his power (Heb. 1.1–4). The Christology of Hebrews is very high. Jesus is depicted as a heavenly figure who occupies a unique position on the scale of being some-where between God and the angels. He is God's only son. We may not have reached a fully Trinitarian position in Hebrews but we are well on the way towards it.

Here, then, we have a portrait of Jesus painted by a Jew, but is it an *authentically* Jewish portrait? The answer to this question is not as obvious as was once thought. There was a time when scholars, even Christian scholars, would have used the high Christology of Hebrews to question its Jewishness. The argument was at bottom simple. Jews, as everyone knows, were and are un-compromising monotheists: after all, the fundamental affirmation of Judaism is found in the Shema which proclaims the uniqueness and the unity of God. So if we find high christological statements in the New Testament then either they cannot mean what they seem to mean (recall the futile attempts to deny that John 1.1 actually implies that the Logos is God), or if they are to be taken at face value, then they are not genuinely Jewish. However, things are not quite so straightforward. We now know that Judaism in the Second Temple period was a highly complex phenomenon, and that some Jewish groups believed in a whole range of heavenly beings who mediated between God and humanity. The Qumran community, for example, had its heavenly high priest called Melchizedek, who would command the forces of light in the final great eschatological war against the forces of darkness led by Belial or the Devil. Hebrews clearly echoes these ideas when it says that Jesus was a heavenly high priest 'after the order of Melchizedek', though it also subtly affirms that as 'son of God' he was superior to Melchizedek. Hebrews for all its high Christology fits rather neatly into one strand of Second Temple Judaism. It is a Jewish portrait of Jesus.

Abraham Geiger

Jewish interest in Jesus has burgeoned in modern times as a direct result of Jewish emancipation and Jewish scholars have increasingly played a part in the search for a historical and critical understanding of Jesus. One of the first figures in this new wave of Jewish engagement with Jesus was the great German Jewish scholar Abraham Geiger (1810–74). Geiger was a leader of Reform Judaism in Germany and a radical thinker. He was among the first of a long line of modern Jewish writers who sought to reclaim Jesus for Judaism. He argued that Jesus had, in fact, said nothing new, that he was a pious and God-fearing Jew who never intended to break with Judaism. The historically authentic Jewish Jesus had been overlaid, by Paul and others, with layer upon layer of in-authentically Jewish varnish. Geiger sets Jesus firmly within a carefully crafted historical reconstruction of Second Temple Judaism, of which the Pharisees are the undoubted leaders and heroes (and the forerunners of nineteenth-century Reform!).[5]

However, as Susannah Heschel has shown in her fascinating study *Abraham Geiger and the Jewish Jesus*,[6] Geiger's account of Jesus cannot be divorced from the history of the nineteenth century and the changing situation of the Jews in Europe. Geiger's appropriation of Jesus served direct political ends. It reminded the Christian majority that in fact Jesus was a Jew, which was of use in raising the status of Jews in Christian eyes. By inserting Jesus firmly into the world of early Judaism, and above all by bringing him into relationship with the classic Rabbinic sources, he at the same time inserted Jews and Judaism into the main-stream of European culture. He established an unbreakable association between them and Europe's supreme cultural icon, Jesus Christ. But at the same time he subtly but provocatively asserted the independence of Judaism by claiming that the Church had actually got it all wrong and falsified the message of Jesus. Geiger was even not averse to invoking Jesus to support his own calls for the Reform of Judaism in his own days. It was a nuanced but fiercely polemical position, which was to set the framework for most subsequent Jewish treatments of Jesus.

Joseph Klausner

Another influential Jewish writer on Jesus was Joseph Klausner. Klausner, who was born in 1874 and died in 1958, was one of the leading Jewish intellectuals of the twentieth century. Born and reared in Lithuania, and educated in Germany (he earned a doctorate at the University of Heidelberg), Klausner ended his life as a distinguished professor of the newly founded Hebrew University of Jerusalem. In 1922 he published the first serious study of Jesus in Hebrew entitled, *Yeshu ha-Notzri: Zemanno, Hayyav ve-Torato* ('Jesus of Nazareth: His times, his life and his Torah'). The work was translated into English by the great Anglican Hebraist and translator of the Mishnah, Herbert Danby, who knew Klausner well from his time as a canon of St George's Cathedral in Jerusalem.[7] Klausner's work was widely read by Christian scholars, who particularly appreciated the ready access it gave them to Rabbinic sources, but it can really only be understood in its Hebrew context.

Klausner's study of Jesus was addressed primarily to Jews, and one of its aims was to offer them a more sympathetic account of Jesus. The search for historical verisimilitude was very much part of the portrait which Klausner attempted to paint. With reference to the birth and infancy of Jesus it is worthwhile noting that Klausner's work had a substantial section entitled 'The Childhood and Youth of Jesus'.[8] However, it begins forthrightly by asserting 'Jesus was born in the reign of Augustus two to four years before the Christian era in the small town of Galilee called Nazareth'. Klausner dismissed the association of Jesus' birth with Bethlehem as clearly motivated by a later concern reflected in Matthew and Luke to propound the theory that as the Messiah Jesus must be a son of David and Bethlehemite. In a similar vein he puts to one side the virginal conception by the Holy Spirit as illogical since, if Jesus had no human father, he really could not have had any connection at all with the house of David. 'Jesus' father was Joseph and his mother Mary.'[9] Beyond these comments there is a brief creative reconstruction of Jesus' childhood in Nazareth, including details concerning his likely education, but from a historian's perspective these early years are best understood through comparison with Hillel the Elder about whose early life even less in known than for the life of Jesus. The significance of both figures comes as they begin to play an active public role.

In addressing his work chiefly to a Jewish audience Klausner, like Geiger, regards Jesus as basically a pious Jew and saw the Jesus of Christianity as essentially a creation of Paul: he argued the latter view at greater length in another Hebrew monograph, *Mi-Yeshu 'ad Paulus* ('From Jesus to Paul'). But unlike Geiger Klausner is prepared to see Jesus in some sense as a radical religious innovator. He included a chapter in his Jesus book entitled, 'Points of Opposition between Judaism and the Teaching of Jesus'. The formulation is interesting. We find it again in the title of the American scholar E. P. Sanders' influential book *Jesus and Judaism*.[10] But it is flawed: it begs a fundamental question by implying that one can, historically, somehow or other set 'Jesus' over against 'Judaism' and compare and contrast the two, whereas Jesus was, by definition, a part of Judaism and since he clearly never rejected his ancestral religion he cannot be set up in opposition to it. To do so would involve a highly dubious essentialising of Judaism.

What Klausner found most disturbing about Jesus was that he was not entirely sound on the Jewish national question. Though he was himself 'undoubtedly a "nationalist" Jew by instinct and even an extreme nationalist',[11] his attitude towards the Jewish ceremonial laws carried dangers. Jesus

> fails to see the national aspect of the ceremonial laws. He never actually sets them aside but he adopts towards them an attitude as to outworn scraps of the new 'messianic garment', and depreciates their religious and moral worth; he does not recognise the connexion which exists between national and human

history, and he entirely lacks the wider political perspective shown by the Prophets, whose sweeping vision embraced kingdoms and nations the world over. Hence all unwittingly, he brought it to pass that part of the 'House of Jacob' was swallowed up by those other nations who, at first, had joined themselves to that part.[12]

Though Jesus was a great moral teacher, whose moral code, if it could be stripped of its 'wrappings of miracles and mysticism', would be 'one of the choicest treasures of the literature of Israel for all time',[13] he failed to see that 'a people does not endure on a foundation of general faith and morality; it needs a "practical religiousness", a ceremonial form of religion which shall embody religious ideas and also crown everyday life with a halo of sanctity'.[14] Klausner's Zionist concerns are barely concealed here. He and others, such as Ahad ha-ʿAm, were exercised by the problem of how to create a Jewish national culture in a restored Jewish state. Like Ahad ha-ʿAm, Klausner saw traditional Jewish custom and practice as having an important role to play in the Jewish culture of that new state. To treat those customs in a cavalier fashion was a cardinal error, which explains how from the teachings of Jesus the Jew 'non-Judaism' arose.[15]

Geza Vermes

The final Jewish scholar whom I would like briefly to mention is Geza Vermes. Vermes, a pioneering student of the Dead Sea Scrolls and of the history of Second Temple Judaism, has had a life-long fascination with Jesus. His trilogy, *Jesus the Jew, Jesus and the World of Judaism* and *The Religion of Jesus the Jew* has recently been supplemented by an important study entitled *The Changing Faces of Jesus*,[16] which traces the transformation of Jesus from a Jewish teacher into the Christ and God of Christendom. Together these constitute the most imposing account of Jesus to date from a Jewish perspective. Vermes' position is nuanced and learned and it is impossible to do it justice in a sentence or two. However, in its broad outlines it stands within the tradition of Geiger and

Klausner. Jesus was a pious, first-century Jew who had no inten-
tion of founding a Church or of breaking with Judaism. Like
Klausner, Vermes, engaged as he is in an historical investigation,
is dismissive of the birth and infancy narratives of Matthew and
Luke, preferring to concentrate on what he labels 'the main
Gospel',[17] the narrative of Jesus' life from his time with John the
Baptist until the discovery of his empty tomb, the Gospel as found
chiefly in Mark.

Vermes' distinctive contribution is to locate Jesus more precisely on the map of Second Temple Judaism, 'not among the
Pharisees, Essenes, Zealots or Gnostics', but among 'the holy
miracle workers of Galilee', such as Honi the Circle-Drawer and
Haninah ben Dosa.[18] Jesus regarded himself as having a close,
filial relationship to God his heavenly father, and as bringing to
Israel a prophetic message of social justice for the marginalised
and oppressed. 'The prophets spoke on behalf of the honest poor,
and defended the widows and the fatherless, those oppressed and
exploited by the wicked, rich and powerful. Jesus went further. In
addition to proclaiming these blessed, he actually took his stand
among the pariahs of his world, those despised by the respectable.
Sinners were his table-companions and the ostracised tax-collectors
and prostitutes his friends.'[19] But he remained firmly within the
boundaries of first-century Palestinian Jewish piety. He did not
regard himself as a messiah, though the role was thrust upon him
early by his followers. His death was a tragedy – a case of being in
the wrong place at the wrong time.

Vermes clearly means to offer a Jewish portrait of Jesus, and he
weaves Jesus skilfully and inextricably into the tapestry of early
Judaism. Indeed he implies that Jesus can only be truly known
from a Jewish standpoint. Note the provocative claim with
which he ends the preface to the first paperback edition of *Jesus
the Jew*:

> Martin Buber, one of the foremost religious thinkers of this
> century and a great admirer of Jesus wrote: 'We Jews know him
> in a way – in the impulses and emotions of his essential
> Jewishness – that remains inaccessible to the Gentiles subject to

him.' . . . I trust that those who accompany me on this voyage
of exploration will recognize the truth of Buber's words.[20]

The picture is compelling and has been influential, but is it an
authentically Jewish portrait of Jesus? And to what extent does it
reflect personal concerns? Vermes himself, as he tells us engag-
ingly in his autobiography, *Providential Accidents*,[21] has had a
remarkable spiritual odyssey, which has ranged from an assimilated Jewish childhood in Hungary and a formal conversion to
Christianity, through a deep commitment to Christianity, training
at the Catholic University of Louvain and membership of the
Fathers of Zion, to an eventual return later in life to his ancestral
faith. To what extent these experiences have coloured his portrait
of Jesus cannot be pursued here, but that they may have should
cause little surprise.

Conclusions

In this short essay I have concentrated on posing rather than
answering questions. Two observations will suffice to bring it to a
close.

First, it is difficult, if not impossible, to obtain an objective
portrait of Jesus. All portraits, whatever their medium, inevitably
reflect the standpoint from which they are observed. Jesus has
been the supreme cultural icon of Europe for the past millennium,
but like all great cultural icons he can become a mirror in which
human aspirations and desires are reflected. Icons religiously are
intended to change the observer. The believer who looks at the
face of Christ is supposed to be transferred into the image of
Christ. What may just as readily happen is that Christ becomes
transformed into the image of the observer. And this is as true in
'objective' scholarship as it is in the lives of 'simple' Christians. As
someone remarked in response to the plethora of books on Jesus,
all of them different, 'By their lives of Christ shall ye know them!'
We need not be too alarmed at this, or too cynical. One's personal
experiences are an essential hermeneutical resource. It is only when

the subject is viewed from different standpoints that its complexity can be fully disclosed.

Second, there is no single authentic Jewish portrait of Jesus, any more than there is a single authentic Christian portrait of Jesus. All the Jewish portraits of Jesus which we have considered are authentic: all acknowledge Jesus as Jewish and attempt to relate him to the Judaism of his day. To designate only one of them as the authentic Jewish portrait involves essentialising one particular strand of Jewish tradition. This is not to suggest that all the portraits are equally historically true, though the tendency in most Jewish portraits to say little about the birth and infancy of Jesus reflects an impressive and earnest concern to investigate the man behind the legend. The questions of historicity and Jewishness should be kept strictly apart. One account may well be closer to the actual historical Jesus than another. But that will have to be decided on the basis of the historical evidence and not on the grounds of its supposed intrinsic Jewishness. Likewise, the Jewishness of Jesus, however that may be conceived, is barely discernible at all in the stories of his birth.

Suggested further reading

SUSANNAH HESCHEL, *Abraham Geiger and the Jewish Jesus* (Chicago and London: University of Chicago Press, 1998).

GEZA VERMES, *The Changing Faces of Jesus* (London: Allen Lane, The Penguin Press, 2000).

CHAPTER TWO

QUMRAN: THE CRADLE OF THE CHRIST?

George J. Brooke

Introduction

There are three principal ways in which the similarities between some of the Dead Sea Scrolls from Qumran and some of the writings of the New Testament can be explained. The first two can be stated very directly and in so doing their probable shortcomings are all the more obvious. Some have maintained, much to the delight of the media, that what was taking place at Qumran provided the cradle from which early Christianity was born and a very few have baldly argued that Jesus himself was either wholly or in part both brought up in and lived as a member of the movement of which the Qumran community was the headquarters. Ernest Renan's oft-quoted statement that Christianity is an Essenism which has largely succeeded[1] is made specific through a reading of the Qumran scrolls. A combination of ignoring some problematic details and of exercising overly vivid imaginations has resulted in a hybrid Jesus less credible than ever.

Yet others have insisted that the differences are so great between what we can learn from the scrolls of the community which collected them and the early Christian records of Jesus and the movement he founded that there can be no way of drawing a relationship between them. On the one hand the key characteristics of Qumran Essenism are priestly purity, a determined protection of sacred space, hard-line legal interpretation, all produced by a

23

group which is the product of the educated urban élite, principally
from Jerusalem. On the other hand, Jesus is from a lower-middle-
class small town family whose ministry shows him to have an
affinity with country folk. His table fellowship is open and notably
scandalous. Though he seems to gravitate towards Jerusalem, he
does so not out of concern to support its institutions, but on the
basis of some eschatological fervour which, as Josephus and others
have let us see for a very long time, was all too common in Palestine
at the time. The Qumran scrolls can only add minimally to the
general picture; they cannot help us in any detailed way to
appreciate better the historical or other concerns of the New
Testament authors.

The third way of relating the evidence of the scrolls to the
evidence of the New Testament about Jesus is more difficult to
characterise as it takes many forms and is often presented in a
nuanced way. The similarities between the two bodies of approx-
imately contemporary literature cannot be reduced to identity,
but neither can the differences force us to dismiss them as insig-
nificant. Something has to be said, for example, about how in the
whole of Jewish literature between the Bible and the Mishnah, it
is only in 4Q521 and the Jesus saying in the double tradition (Q)
of Luke and Matthew that Isaiah 61.1–2 is expanded with a
statement about the raising of the dead.[2] 'He will heal the wounded,
and revive the dead and bring good news to the poor' says 4Q521;
'the dead are raised, the poor have good news brought to them'[3]
echoes Luke (Q) 7.22 as Jesus answers the disciples of John the
Baptist concerning himself. Whether we conclude that Jesus must
have known of this tradition directly from a Qumran source[4] or
that it was mediated to him in some other way, the details of the
similarities are too great to be brushed aside.

Some resonances between the Dead Sea Scrolls and the Gospel birth narratives

In this short essay I wish to look briefly at four items from the
Qumran scrolls which have resonances with the birth of Jesus

and its associated narratives. The discussion will show some of the varying ways in which the third way of trying to relate the Scrolls and the New Testament literature may be suitably undertaken.

Son of God and Son of the Most High

The first item is not unlike the parallel between 4Q521 and Luke (Q) 7.22. 4Q246 is officially labelled an Aramaic Apocryphon of Daniel.[5] A single substantial fragment (14 × 9 cms) of this first-century BC manuscript survives; it comes from the end of a sheet of leather. The first column of nine lines is extant only at its left side; the second column is completely preserved, but the text must have continued on to another column on a further sheet of leather. From the broken context of the first column it seems as if an interpreter, possibly Daniel, comes before a king to explain a vision which the king has seen. In addition to the kings of Assyria and Egypt, the interpreter describes another royal figure who clearly belongs to the future. The line is broken but the surviving words can be translated as '. . . great he will be called and by his name will he be surnamed'. At the top of the second column the interpreter declares: 'He will be called the Son of God and the Son of the Most High they will name him.' The text continues by describing the rule of the kings as a time of great turmoil when peoples and provinces destroy one another. This violence is followed by an epoch when the people of God will arise and there will be peace. The eternal kingdom which ensues is characterised by truth and righteousness. It is difficult to determine whether or not the last king of the three mentioned, the Son of God and the Son of the Most High, is the king of God's people during this time.

The difficulties in making sense of the text have provoked a wide range of scholarly interpretations. Some have suggested that all three kings are to be viewed negatively and that the last is an antichrist or an actual ruler of Judaea who was viewed in a very poor light by the author of the composition since he has taken

the titles Son of God and Son of the Most High unlawfully. Others
have argued that the third king is to be associated with the people
of God in a positive way and that he is to be understood as either
a messianic figure or a guardian archangel who fights on Israel's
behalf.[6]

Whatever the case with the correct understanding of 4Q246,
four striking parallels with Luke 1.32–35 emerge. In Luke Gabriel's
message to Mary is divided into two parts. Together with other
details, in Luke 1.30–33 he describes the one who will be named
Jesus, who will be great, called Son of the Most High, whose
kingdom will have no end. In the second part of the message
(Luke 1.35–37), in answer to Mary's question 'How can this be?'
Gabriel states that the Holy Spirit will come upon her and the
power of the Most High will overshadow her so that the child
will be holy and called Son of God. Jesus will be great, he is to be
Son of the Most High, to have an eternal kingdom, and to be
called Son of God.

When one or two of the same motifs occur in two different
passages, it is necessary to exercise caution. When the same four
items occur in a few lines in one text and in as many verses in
another, some kind of explanation is called for. It is clear that the
language of various Danielic traditions is reflected in both 4Q246
and Luke 1.32–37. Most especially there are echoes of Daniel 2.44:
'And in the days of those kings the God of heaven will set up a
kingdom that shall never be destroyed, nor shall this kingdom
be left to another people. It shall crush all these kingdoms and
bring them to an end, and it shall stand forever.' Daniel 7.27 also
comes to mind: 'The kingship and dominion and the greatness
of the kingdoms under the whole heaven shall be given to the
people of the holy ones of the Most High; their kingdom shall be
an everlasting kingdom, and all dominions shall serve and obey
them.'

While it is possible that both 4Q246 and Luke 1 are independent
meditations on Danielic promises, it seems preferable to consider
seriously that Luke 1 was dependent on some such tradition as
is found in 4Q246 and that whoever compiled Gabriel's message

to Mary understood the third king mentioned in 4Q246 in a positive way as the individual personification of the eschatological rule of the people of God. There are no explicit hints that the third king in 4Q246 has Davidic features, but the author of Luke 1 provided them to complete his positive reading of his source: 'the Lord God will give to him the throne of his ancestor David' (Luke 1.32). The parallel between 4Q246 and Luke 1.32–37 indicates to the modern interpreter that the description of the birth and naming of Jesus is one way of reading a polyvalent Jewish tradition.

The woman in travail

The second item is a piece of narrative poetry. One of the first manuscripts to come to light from Cave 1 is a copy of a set of thanksgiving hymns (in Hebrew, *Hodayot*). It is widely and very suitably supposed that one of the leading figures in the community at some point wrote several of these hymns as reflections upon his own experiences. These poems have an autobiographical feel to them. Detailed studies of stylistic consistency and vocabulary usage suggest that even if the poems cannot be attributed directly to the community's Teacher of Righteousness, at least they form a coherent body of verse authored almost certainly by a single person.

In what is now designated as column 11 of the Thanksgiving Hymn scroll there is a poem which is so tightly expressed that it is extremely difficult to translate. Almost every phrase is replete with double meanings.

> I am in distress, like a woman in labor with her firstborn when her travail begins, when the mouth of her womb pulses with agony, when the firstborn of the woman writhes within her. Surely children come forth through the breakers of death, and she who gives a man birth suffers agonies!
>
> Yet through the breakers of death she delivers a male child, and through hellish agonies bursts forth from the bearer's womb: a Wonderful Counsellor with His mighty power!

> But when the man comes safely through the breakers, they
> all rush upon his bearer: grievous agonies strike those giving
> birth, terrors come to their mothers. When he is born, the
> travails all turn back on the bearer's womb.[7]

The author likens his psychological and possibly also his physical
sufferings to a woman giving birth. And when the male firstborn
child is safely delivered, the poet continues to belabour his point
and his agonies continue in the afterbirth. The one born is the
wonderful mighty counsellor, words that are borrowed from Isaiah
9.6: 'For a child has been born for us, a son given to us; authority
rests upon his shoulders; and he is named Wonderful Counsellor,
Mighty God, Everlasting Father, Prince of Peace.' Isaiah speaks
of a coming king who will occupy the throne of David. The
Qumran poet noticeably stops short of referring to God in his
allusion to Isaiah 9.6 or of developing the royal imagery with
reference to a kingly messiah. Since it is clear that the poet likens
himself to the woman in travail, I am inclined to believe that the
child born is representative of the community for which the poet
considered himself as a parent.[8] The messianic language of Isaiah
thus has a corporate significance.

Three small matters seem to confirm this view. First, the
term used for the one delivered is *geber*, 'man', a Hebrew word
used exclusively of human offspring; so the offspring must be
considered fully human. Second, there is a delightful possibility in the phrase 'Wonderful Counsellor with his mighty
power' of reading the two consonants translated usually as the
preposition 'with' ('*im*) as the noun 'people' ('*am*); the 'wonderful
counsellor is a people of mighty power'. This *double entendre*
would support a corporate reading of the figure. Third, in
another Qumran sectarian composition, the so-called Eschatological Midrash (4Q174), an interpretation of Psalm 2 identifies
the anointed one of the Psalm with the chosen ones of Israel,
namely the community members. Thus what was taken as a
messianic passage in the late Second Temple period was also
capable of being understood corporately with reference to a
select community.

In light of all this we may propose that the poetic birth narrative of 1QH^a 11 urges upon those who reflect on the birth of Jesus to be on the lookout for corporate meanings in the texts, so that his birth is conceived as the birth of all people. Furthermore, as a contemporary literary trope the ongoing agony of the one who gives birth is easily discernible in the one whose soul shall also be pierced (Luke 2.35) or who flees into the wilderness before the dragon (Rev. 12.5–6). Any actual birth of a messianic community is simply the delivery of the divine muse which once found the mind of the Qumran teacher most fertile and conceived there a whole community.

Begetting the Messiah

The third item concerns eschatological hope. There are two appendices to the Cave 1 version of the Rule of the Community (1QS). The first is a two-column rule book for the last days (1QSa) which has become known either as the Rule of the Congregation or occasionally as the Messianic Rule. The closing section of this rule book describes what happens at meals when there are at least ten men gathered together. The manuscript is somewhat damaged with some pieces missing altogether and others barely legible. In places the opening of this final unit of the Rule of the Congregation is both damaged and difficult to read. The part which concerns us for the birth of Jesus is in the title to the section: 'This is the assembly of famous men, [those summoned to] the gathering of the community council, when [God] begets the Messiah with them.'[9] Geza Vermes translates the same significant phrase as 'When God engenders (the Priest-) Messiah' and comments that the reading of *yôlîd*, 'engenders' or 'begets', is confirmed by computer image enhancement.[10] Michael Wise notes the difficulty in the reading here and alongside 'when [God] has fa[th]ered(?) the Messiah' also offers 'when the Messiah has been revealed', based on a recent proposal by Emile Puech who has detected elements of a supralinear letter which adjusts the final contentious word of the line.[11]

This manuscript is regularly dated to the first quarter of the first century BC. It raises the question whether a Jewish text of that time really speaks of God begetting the Messiah. Sadly the leather is badly darkened at the end of the line just where the crucial word occurs and the beginning of the next line where one would expect to find the subject of that verb mentioned is missing. Thus, if the subject of the verb at the end of the line was God, then sadly he is a hidden God. Perhaps not surprisingly, several Jewish scholars tend to prefer alternative readings and restorations here, such as that by Jacob Licht, taken up by Lawrence Schiffman: 'when [at the end] (of days) the messiah [shall assemble] with them'.[12] Some other scholars have offered alternative suggestions too, such as 'when the Messiah has been revealed', as has already been mentioned. The majority, however, from the first attempts to be sure about the reading which was published in the official edition of the manuscript in 1955 until the most recent edition of the Hebrew text by Florentino García Martínez in 1997, have dared to read *yôlîd*, 'begets' or 'engenders', and have understood the passage to be about the divine parenting of the Messiah.[13]

Given such a reading, it would be unwise to think that this Jewish text from about 100 BC was referring to a virgin birth. Rather, in line with a biblical text such as 2 Samuel 7.14, the text can be considered as endorsing a particularly intimate relationship between God and the anointed king. What are the implications for the New Testament birth narratives of this reading and understanding of the Rule of the Congregation 2.11–12? Of primary importance must be the way in which metaphor takes priority over literalness. If the Qumran text expresses no concern for how the divine parenthood of the messiah came about, it is because the assumption must be that he had good Jewish parents and was fully human; no contemporary Jewish texts would suggest otherwise. In Luke and Matthew, therefore, the priority of metaphor has been misplaced and a proof text from the Greek translation of Isaiah 7.14 introduced. That proof text has ever since held the doctrine of the full humanity of Jesus to ransom.

Praising God's greatness

The fourth item helps us to see that those who reflected on the birth of Jesus recognised that something of the creative strength of God was at work in what had taken place. Several of the scrolls from Qumran contain compositions which are slightly reworked forms of the biblical books as we know them today. It is clear that before each book of the Bible had a fixed text form, those who viewed them as authoritative copied them not in the idolatrous fashion which is worship of the letter without recognition of the meaning, but rather as writings which were of continuing living significance to be ever improved in minor ways so that God's purposes for Israel contained in them could be heard all the more readily in each successive generation. One of these reworked biblical paraphrases is known to Qumran scholars as the Reworked Pentateuch. This survives in several copies; it is the one labelled 4Q365 which concerns us here.

The so-called Reworked Pentateuch follows what is now contained in the traditional text of the Hebrew Bible very closely for the most part. However, from time to time there are some significant differences from what is now accepted as canonical by Jews and most Christians alike. At Exodus 15 the manuscript is poorly preserved, but enough survives for us to know that before Exodus 15.22–26, which is represented almost as in the traditional Hebrew Bible, there was a narrative poem. Sadly the damage to the manuscript only allows us to read a few opening words on each line. What is preserved reads as follows:

> you despised (?) [
> for the majesty of [
> You are great, a deliverer (?) [
> the hope of the enemy has perished, and he is for[gotten]
>   (or: has cea[sed])
> they perished in the mighty waters, the enemy
>   (or 'enemies') [
> Extol the one who raises up, [a r]ansom . . . you gave (?) [
> [the one who do]es gloriously [[14]

In these tantalising lines, there seems to be preserved the song which Miriam sang as the counterpart to that which Moses and the male Israelites had sung after safely crossing the sea (Exod. 15.1–18). In the Bible as we have it, Miriam is given the opening verse of the Song of the Sea to sing. Exodus 15.1 is repeated by her almost verbatim in Exodus 15.21. It is as if she then goes on to repeat the whole song in imitation of Moses and the men, as their faithful echo. In this Reworked Pentateuch composition, rather than being a mere echo, she seems to have her own song to sing. A few of the words which survive, such as 'mighty waters' (cf. Exod. 15.10), suitably take up the motifs of the Song of the Sea, but overall Miriam's song is different, a distinctive song for a woman.[15]

The surviving text is frustratingly fragmentary, but two motifs are striking. First, Miriam addresses God directly as great, a deliverer. The address 'You are great' might at first sight seem a common way for a psalmist to call upon God, but the phrase is surprisingly rare. Its exact equivalent is to be found only in Psalm 86.10, part of a prayer for deliverance from personal enemies, and in the Book of Judith 16.13. Judith 16.1–17 is a victory song which Judith sings after the divine defeat of Holofernes and the Babylonian army through her powerless agency: 'The Lord almighty has foiled them by the hand of a woman' (Judith 16.5). The second noteworthy motif in the new Song of Miriam is how the sixth line contains a reference to exaltation. It seems as if the phrase exhorts the hearer to extol God who raises somebody up. What the original context contained can only be guessed at. Perhaps there was a reference to the way God had raised up a downtrodden and nearly defeated Israel. For our purposes it is this very activity of God which exemplifies his greatness. The very same combination of motifs is found in the victory song of another Mary in Luke 1.46–55: 'My soul magnifies the Lord . . . He has lifted up the lowly.'

Some modern commentators might wish to propose that this new Song of Miriam was very old and had long been part of the narrative of Exodus before some scribe dared to replace it with the opening verse of the male chorus. I suspect the song is secondary. It seems to be another example of the kind of victory songs which are attributed to women in the late Second Temple period. Indeed it could well be a second-century BC composition, like the song in Judith 16. Some have argued that Mary's Magnificat is the adaptation of a Jewish victory song from the Maccabean period.[16] If so, then all three songs would be roughly contemporary. In these songs we can see clearly that it is permissible for women to sing of the victorious greatness of God, to admit their frailty in all things and to acknowledge forcefully that it is God alone who raises up the lowly.

Conclusion

The Qumran texts show us what was conceivable in Judaism at the time. Our four texts make significant contributions to the better appreciation of the Gospel birth narratives. In light of 4Q246 we can see that the stories of the birth of Jesus were but one or more ways of reading polyvalent Jewish tradition. On the basis of the Thanksgiving Hymn we note that the narrative allows for a corporate understanding so that it is legitimate to consider that all people can receive their identity through this one illegitimate birth. The Rule of the Congregation shows that it is not scandalous to talk of divine parenthood providing that metaphor takes priority over literal explanation. The Song of Miriam shows us that some aspects of God's power are most readily visible when sung about by a woman. Thus the manuscripts from Qumran provide us with several of the planks that make up the cradle of the Christ. But much of its overall structure and the baby it cradles are strictly speaking from another carpenter's shop altogether.

Suggested further reading

KLAUS BERGER, *The Truth under Lock and Key? Jesus and the Dead Sea Scrolls* (Louisville, KY: Westminster John Knox Press, 1995).

RAYMOND E. BROWN, *A Coming Christ in Advent: Essays on the Gospel Narratives Preparing for the Birth of Jesus (Matthew 1 and Luke 1)* (Collegeville, MN: The Liturgical Press, 1988).

JAMES H. CHARLESWORTH and WILLIAM P. WEAVER (eds), *The Dead Sea Scrolls and the Christian Faith: In Celebration of the Jubilee Year of the Discovery of Qumran Cave 1* (Harrisburg, PA: Trinity Press International; London: SCM Press, 1998).

JAMES C. VANDERKAM, *The Dead Sea Scrolls Today* (Grand Rapids, MI: Eerdmans; London: SPCK, 1994).

CHAPTER THREE

UNCOVERING THE CORONA:
A THEOLOGY OF CIRCUMCISION

Graham Ward

Circumcision: the body politic

I have it from the historian of homosexuality, David Greenberg, on the basis of medical statistics since the passing of public health legislation in the United States before the Second World War, that the majority of American men are circumcised at birth. In fact, to be an uncircumcised American man is unusual and attracts attention in those various areas where men become, often uncomfortably, aware of bodies of other men, particularly other naked men. The reason why this pan-circumcision takes place has nothing to do with Judaism or Christianity. The foreskin is viewed as the potential harbourer of certain infections. Since most babies are born in hospital, it is medically and politically more economical to deal with what is, after all, only an excess of tissue, while the aforesaid male baby is on-site. Circumcision has undergone a definite desacralisation.

But, as far as I can see, circumcision has been not only a biological but a political issue throughout, if only as a marker of those who belong and those who are excluded. The politics change with each cultural context. While the act (the removal of the foreskin from around the penile helmet) has remained the same, the way that act is understood and evaluated shifts continually. Despite cultural fashion concerning shape and size and piercings, a penis is a penis. The technology for accomplishing the act of

circumcision has also changed; and likewise the interpretation of
the act and the events itself have changed. It is how theology is
implicated in this politics that interests me in this essay.

The account of the circumcision of Jesus is not without its
own politics. In what follows I wish to give two examples of this
and raise the question as to what these politics can indicate in two
different cultural situations.

The circumcision of Jesus: sharpening the issues

My first example is the account of the circumcision itself in Luke's
Gospel, and my first question about this account concerns why it
occurs only in Luke's Gospel. What does this signify? Mark's
Gospel has no infancy narrative and so the lack of any reference
to Jesus' circumcision is readily explicable. John's Gospel contains
a reference to circumcision (John 7.22–23), but not an account of
Jesus' own. Of course, it could be argued that since there is, at
best, only a veiled reference to the birth of Jesus in the prologue
of John's Gospel (John 1.14), as in the case of Mark's Gospel
there is no narrative necessity for mentioning the circumcision.
But something must be said about Matthew. Whilst I am no New
Testament scholar, the little work on the New Testament I have
done points to how Matthew's Gospel has an implied Jewish
reader.[1] It is a Gospel also with an infancy narrative and a concern
to show Jesus as the fulfilment of Jewish law and prophecy. Luke's
Gospel, on the other hand, has an implied Graeco-Roman reader,
being addressed to Gentile converts with little or no background
knowledge in Judaism but with some Hellenistic education
(various studies have argued that the Greek of Luke's Gospel is
more rhetorically conscious, the vocabulary more sophisticated).
So when the circumcision ought to appear in Matthew's Gospel
to show that this Jesus of Nazareth really did live out the letter of
the Jewish law – it doesn't. It appears in the Gospel addressed to
Gentile outsiders. Why is this? Or more accurately, why might
this be – for we are not going to resolve how to interpret this issue
today, or ever?

Let me suggest that what is missing, present or elaborated in any of the Gospel accounts of the life of Jesus is governed not simply by a theological project but also by a cultural politics. In fact, the theologies propounded in whatever context are both the product and the producer of specific cultural forces. That is, if we view every culture as a set of interrelated symbolic systems, establishing values here, legitimating certain forms of activity there, negatively judging or downgrading opposing values, criminalising forms of activity inconsistent with the kinds of living endorsed, then within the overlapping of those symbolic codes certain symbols are given more priority than others. Certain symbols are key symbols used to interpret or order other lesser valued symbols.[2] Each person internalises this priority, this hierarchy, often without reflection. In this way specific cultural ideologies become normative. Each person then reproduces, modifies, even possibly critiques such priorities and hierarchies in the various practices which make up the everyday living within any particular culture. I suggest that Luke is doing the same with the circumcision, that circumcision becomes not the organising and key symbol but one which, in the cultural milieu in which Luke's Gospel was composed, took on a certain weight, a significance which it did not have in the cultural milieu of the Johannine community, for example, or the cultural context in which both Mark and Matthew were writing. The circumcision was important for Luke and significant with respect to the culture he was addressing – and I want to know why. I want to understand the cultural politics, the movement of social energies which leads Luke to write this scene into his account of the life of Jesus.

It is a scene given a certain rhetorical prominence. For not only does it parallel and repeat (albeit differently) the circumcision and naming of John the Baptist (Luke 1.59), but it acts as a tiny bridge between two large pericopes, the nativity (Luke 2.1–20; where narrative attention is drawn to the pastoral framing and that which Mary kept pondering 'in her heart') and the presentation in the Temple (Luke 2.22–40; where Simeon prophesies the piercing of Mary's soul in the context of sacrifice). The circumcision links salvation to naming and sacrifice, weaving a complex relation between Mary and the Christ. For the cutting Jesus undergoes is a cutting Mary herself undergoes in her own soul too: 'a sword will pierce through your soul *also*' (*de*; Luke 2.35). The present event of circumcision dissolves into the future prophecy while it floats upon a past resonant with connotations of shepherd kings and sacrificial lambs. Time is being governed; an explicit sense of providence is performed through certain symmetries: John with Jesus; Jesus with Mary. The brief action takes on a symbolic weight, a diaphanous quality – as if when held up to the sunlight of eternal truth the watermark of what has been and what will come permeates its present significance.

I am unconvinced by those who might say this inclusion of the circumcision in Luke's Gospel was an early example of what we have come to term Orientalism: a westerner employing certain westernised views of eastern practices in order to add a bit of local colour or novelistic realism. Of course, it is one of several references by Luke to Jesus' conformity with the Jewish law. That is its theological *raison d'être*. But what I am suggesting is that it is at the same time an event with specific cultural resonance of which we today register the reverberations, but with which we know not how to proceed. What does it mean for Jesus as incarnate God to have the foreskin of his penis removed? What did it mean for Gentile Christians, what did it signify to those whom the Gospel according to Luke was read? We know from the Book of Acts and the Pauline Epistles the difficulties the circumcision of Jesus caused to those Gentile converts. Furthermore, as Daniel Boyarin argues, 'For the Jews of late antiquity, I claim, the rite of circumcision became the most contested site . . . precisely because of the way that it concentrates in one moment representations of the significance of sexuality, genealogy and ethnic specificity in bodily practice.'[3] So what kind of politics was circumcision implicated in?

The circumcision of Jesus in Luke is associated textually with naming, sacrifice and salvation. These themes were taken up and developed by the early Church Fathers like Ambrose and Augustine in their allegorical readings of the circumcision. As such circumcision was related to three sets of issues. First, it was connected with a set of moral dispositions to be imitated by followers of Christ: kenotic obedience, self-denial, renunciation. Second, it was linked to a set of soteriological criteria: the blood-letting as a downpayment for the redemption to follow, a token of the sacrifice on the cross. And third, it was related to a set of eschatological values: the eighth day on which the liturgy proceeded was symbolically linked to the final resurrection (the eighth being the day following the last day in the cosmic calendar). From the early sixth century 1 January became the Feast of the Circumcision in the Christian Church, the great feast (no doubt to replace pagan feasts) between Christmas and Epiphany. And most of the material we have on the theology of circumcision is found in the sermons and homilies preached on this Feast Day. This allegorising of the surgical event was a continuation of Jewish hermeneutical method. Circumcision was already being employed metaphorically to refer to hearts and ears in the Old Testament and no less than Philo in his essay *The Migration of Abraham* proclaimed: 'It is true that receiving circumcision does indeed portray the excision of pleasure and all the passions, and the putting away of the impious conceit, under which the mind supposed that it was capable of begetting by its own power.'[4]

Now all this is very erudite, but let's be clear what we are doing in this allegorical move (and, more generally, in rendering a 'theological interpretation' of a concrete event). An episode in a narrative is suddenly opaque, as if we don't know how to understand the nature of its inclusion. To that opacity we accredit not artistic or creative integrity, but, since we are dealing with a sacred and revelatory text, we accredit it with theological value. That is, we deem its opacity not a case of bad writing nor aesthetic pragmatism (some local colour to make this account believable) nor a chronicler's appendage of another bit of biographical information, but as theologically significant. However, though we deem it significant, we do not quite know of what it is significant. By wheeling in the allegorical interpretations of the

Philos, the Origens and the Gregory the Greats, we are weighing the episode down with symbolic suggestiveness. In other words we are legitimating its significance by an appeal to the way it encodes transhistorical and eternal truths. To employ good Hellenistic vocabulary, we are translating *historia* into *theoria*. By such a move we are announcing that the material becomes densely significant by investing it with eternal verities, ethical normativities and conceptual categories. And then the material as such begins to disappear – just like, in Luke's account, the details of Jesus' circumcision are conspicuous in their absence.

Put crudely, in the hermeneutical move towards moral disposition, soteriology and eschatology, we are no longer talking about the handling and mutilation of sexual organs (and their implication in genealogy and ethnicity). Rather, we are talking about the preparation of the heart or soul for receiving the divine. We are not talking about the cutting of male flesh, pain or soreness and an ethnic boundary marking predicated upon bleeding; we are not talking about the disposal of unwanted body tissue – what does happen to all those foreskins anyway? We are not talking about gendered, ethnic bodies, what we do with them, what we write upon them, and how they are valued or demeaned. We are talking about the transcendent meaning of bodies, eschatological bodies, the resurrection of bodies on the eighth day. And this is not only hermeneutically reductive; it is ethically and theologically suspicious. For we lose embodiment this way: what I do, experience, and live out now in this racial context, as belonging to this sex and this ethnic grouping is read, transcendently, from elsewhere, seen by the eye of God. And from elsewhere, from above, it loses its importance for me now – I who do these things. We are justifying something solely on the account of what it means in another time, in another place.

I want to suggest, however, that the circumcision of Jesus means something which is definable from the here and now and that that too is theologically and ethically important. I want to suggest also that circumcision meant something then to Luke – meant something culturally and politically; it said something about embodiment, something possibly about being male, something about the way certain figurations of the body are invested with cultural status, something about the politics of embodiment. For the body, until its medicalisation and dissection in the late Renaissance and early seventeenth century, was not a discrete entity.[5] It was not only malleable, it was mapped onto and composed other bodies larger than itself – social and political bodies.[6] The body, as early as Plato in *The Republic*, was understood as establishing a hierarchical system of values: physical, political and cosmic. What then does the circumcised body mean when it is conceived as figuring the social and political body, or as an analogue of the cosmic and divine body – not simply a physical (or spiritual) one?

Circumcision: absence and presence in the fourteenth to sixteenth centuries

Let me come now to my second example of the cultural politics of the circumcision of Jesus. This brings us closer to home (historically and geographically) and it gets me out of troubled New Testament waters and the danger of the sharks within those waters ready to take lumps out of unwitting theologians who wander in there untrained, unlettered. The circumcision of Jesus, as already mentioned, has been celebrated by the Church since the sixteenth century, but it enjoyed a certain cultic fashion in the fourteenth, fifteenth and early sixteenth centuries in particular. Suddenly, added to the regular sermons still preached all over Christendom at the opening of the year, collections of orations delivered in the Vatican by aspiring theologians like Campano (in his *De circumcisione*), Carvajal (in his *Oratio in die circumcisionis*), Cardulus (in his *Oratio de circumcisione*) and Lollio (in his *Oratio circumcisionis*) were published. A study of them has been made by the historian of rhetoric John O'Malley.[7] This was the time when Catherine of Siena claimed a betrothal to Christ which was mystically figured as the wearing of her Lord's foreskin as a ring. Several churches in fact claimed to have the perpuce of Christ – most particularly St John Lateran. Since the Feast of the Circumcision took place between Christmas and Epiphany, several painters depicted the purpose of the visitation by the magi as an inspection of the circumcised genitalia of Jesus; this is the case, for example, in both Botticelli's *Adoration of the Magi* (1470) and in Pieter Bruegel's *Adoration of the Magi* (1564).

Now part of what is going on here is a new emphasis upon the incarnational, the human and material significance of God's coming to dwell among his children. Culturally there was a move to humanise the Christ and to live Christ out in the world as St Francis enjoined. As Bernardino Carvajal (preaching before Sextus IV) proclaimed: 'By circumcision he showed himself to be truly incarnate in human flesh.'[8] There was also the continuation of the allegorising of the circumcision, emphasising its relation, in the New Covenant, to baptism, to self-sacrifice, to the glorified and resurrected body.

Furthermore, this revaluation of the circumcision was not just going on at this time among Christians. Elliot Wolfson has demonstrated the way in which the Kabbalists developed what the Old Testament and Mishnah employed as a trope into a mystical symbol. In the *Zohar* circumcision is associated with the ability to see the *Shekhinah*, the divine presence. The circumcision, as an inscription in the flesh of the Hebrew letter *yod* (the first letter of the tetragrammaton) 'represents the divine imprint on the body'. The physical opening, therefore, is the seal that, in its symbolic valence, corresponds to an ontological opening in God.[9] Furthermore, entering the *Shekhinah* is an erotic experience of penetrating the divine feminine. The Kabbalists, if Wolfson is to be believed, related the eye and the penis in an expression of how the initiated had the ability to see mystically and understand; and they related the phallus and the mouth, 'the covenant of the foreskin and the covenant of the tongue'.[10] A secret wisdom is imparted such that 'the process of circumcision, the removal of the foreskin and the uncovering of the corona, is a disclosure of the secret. In the disclosure of the phallus, through the double act of circumcision, the union of the masculine and feminine aspects of God assured'.[11]

But for all this cultural attention to circumcision, whenever the naked member of Jesus was displayed pictorially or in sculpture, it is never a circumcised penis that is revealed. I could show you any number of paintings of naked uncircumcised baby Jesuses by Cariani, dal Colle, Perugino, Conegliano, Corregio and others, in all of which Jesus seems to be well over eight days old. But perhaps more striking are the sculptures of Michaelangelo, especially the Risen Christ and his famous David. Neither of them is circumcised. Now why, in a culture that found great significance in the circumcision, is the circumcision itself not physically portrayed, even when the genitals of Jesus are carefully delineated? Why is circumcision orally and textually proclaimed and physically and visibly masked? What is organising the denial here, just as, with the account in Luke, what is organising the avowal there?

Towards some answers

Now I suppose, having led you this far, you think I am about to present you with the answers. But you are going to be disappointed, for there are only several partial constructions of answers.

A psychoanalytical construction would no doubt associate circumcision with castration and see Luke's account as Jesus' inter-nalisation of, and redemption from, the pain of the castration complex. Similarly, the psychoanalytical account would suggest the arrival of a new male fear of that same complex evident socially and culturally in the late Middle Ages and Renaissance.

But politically I am struck by the rejection of the Jewish body both in the Graeco-Roman period and in Renaissance culture. This rejection gave rise in both periods to persecution and pogroms. Youths being educated in the Hellenistic schools exercise naked and it is recorded that some Hellenised Jews who attended such schools underwent surgery to replace the foreskin (see 1 Macc. 1.15; Josephus, *Antiquities* 12.241; 1 Cor. 7.18). In the Renaissance period circumcision was mainly associated with

Muslims, who were slaves, or with Jews who were associated with the greedy and covetous sides of nascent capitalism. In both cultures the circumcised body is a socially and aesthetically inferior body. In both cultures the circumcised body was a mutilated and wounded body, the kind of body that could not stand for cosmic and political harmony, the correlation of microcosm to macrocosm. Why should the resurrected body of Christ have its foreskin restored?

Let me suggest then that both Luke's inclusion of an account of the circumcision of Jesus (coy as it is on detail) and the dissolution of the physical circumcision in favour of the spiritual in the fourteenth to the sixteenth centuries are both political gestures (of different, maybe opposite kinds) that need further examination. Luke's appears to be a gesture of resistance to the cultural hegemony of Hellenism. Michelangelo's gesture is a capitulation to a cultural hegemony, in which the Jewish body was rendered socially, politically, aesthetically and theologically invisible. An analysis of the cultural politics of embodiment enables us to see, then, how bodies are made and their significance produced, through the abjection of other bodies.

Suggested further reading

DANIEL BOYARIN, *Carnal Israel: Reading Sex in Talmudic Culture* (Berkeley: University of California Press, 1993).

DALE MARTIN, *The Corinthian Body* (New Haven: Yale University Press, 1995).

JONATHAN SAWDAY, *The Body Emblazoned: Dissection and the Human Body in Renaissance Culture* (London: Routledge, 1995).

II

JESUS: FULLY HUMAN AND MORE

CHAPTER FOUR

THE BIRTH OF JESUS
AND WHY PAUL WAS IN FAVOUR OF IT

R. Barry Matlock

Introduction

My title, 'The birth of Jesus and why Paul was in favour of it', is on the model of the old joke about infant baptism: 'Do you believe in infant baptism?' 'Believe in it? Why, I've seen it done!' I am imagining Paul being asked for his thoughts on the birth of Jesus, and him coming out altogether in favour of it – yes, all to the good that Jesus was born, far better than otherwise. The old joke draws such humour as it possesses from the failure of the response to take up the question about infant baptism on quite the desired level. If there is any humour left in my analogous take on Paul and the birth of Jesus after I have explained it, it serves a serious purpose in suggesting possible difficulties, perhaps even disappointment, in our effort to get onto the same level with Paul on the subject of this collection of essays. To back up a bit from such a rush toward my conclusions, and to put it in the form of a question: Do Paul's letters indicate a theological interest in the birth of Jesus? In answering this question, I will briefly survey the relevant Pauline texts, examine claims that have been made on their basis, and draw conclusions for our overall theme of 'the birth of Jesus'.

The Pauline evidence

From the start, our reaction to the very idea of turning to Paul
with our interest in Jesus' birth may well be something like: 'Paul
– what does *he* have to say about it?' But the Pauline letters, in
their own way, speak with a certain eloquence on the matter.
Paul refers a handful of times to what in traditional terms we
might call Jesus' 'advent' or 'incarnation'.[1] Quite striking are
instances where Jesus is imaged as simply arriving on the human
scene. Thus Romans 8.3: 'For God has done what the law,
weakened by the flesh, could not do: by sending his own Son in
the likeness of sinful flesh, and to deal with sin, he condemned
sin in the flesh . . .'; and 2 Corinthians 8.9: 'For you know the
generous act of our Lord Jesus Christ, that though he was rich,
yet for your sakes he became poor, so that by his poverty you
might become rich.'[2] We may also include here 2 Corinthians
5.21: 'For our sake he made him to be sin who knew no sin, so
that in him we might become the righteousness of God'; compare
Galatians 3.13, Christ's 'becoming a curse for us', and the 'advent'
language of Galatians 3, the 'coming' of (metaphorically) 'the seed'
(v. 19) or (by metonymy) 'faith' (vv. 23, 25). In each of these
instances, Jesus' appearance is quite abrupt, and the effect, perhaps,
is to render this character somewhat mysterious – a motif given
concrete literary form in Mark's Gospel, where, notoriously, Jesus
just walks fully-formed onto the world stage ('In those days Jesus
came from Nazarath of Galilee and was baptised by John in the
Jordan', Mark 1.9).

Now Mark's indirect reference to Jesus' mother, brothers and
sisters (Mark 6.1–3) is enough – if common sense alone does not
suffice – for us to infer an awareness that Jesus didn't really just
pop up out of nowhere. Paul does us one better and actually
mentions the birth of Jesus, two or three times, in fact. In Galatians
4.4–5: 'when the fullness of time had come, God sent his Son,
born of a woman, born under the law, in order to redeem those
under the law . . .'; in Romans 1.3–4: 'the gospel concerning [God's]
Son, who was descended from David [literally 'born of the seed

of David'[3]] according to the flesh and was declared to be Son of God with power according to the spirit of holiness by resurrection from the dead . . .'; and in Philippians 2.7: 'Christ Jesus . . . emptied himself, taking the form of a slave, being born in human likeness.' But somehow in all three of these cases, mention of Jesus' birth notwithstanding, Paul's attention seems to be decidedly elsewhere. 'Born of woman' in Galatians 4.4 seems simply to speak stereotypically of Jesus' humanity. And much the same goes for Romans 1.3 and Philippians 2.7: it is surely Jesus' identity, in humiliation and exaltation, that is of interest, not the circumstances of his birth *as such*. We weren't necessarily expecting shepherds or magi, angelic visitations or wandering stars, the heavenly hosts or the slaughter of the innocents. But Paul seems to have pared the birth of Jesus down to the bare fact of its occurrence. So far, then, Paul does not seem to hold out much promise for our theme of 'the birth of Jesus'.

More than meets the eye?

But not everyone sees it so; or rather, it is claimed that there is more here than meets the eye. David Wenham, in his important and wide-ranging study *Paul: Follower of Jesus or Founder of Christianity?*, raises the question of how much Paul knew of the pre-passion *story*, the narrative tradition of Jesus – beginning with the birth narratives.[4] Notice already that the question must assume an early narrative tradition of Jesus' birth, and this has at least two weighty considerations against it from the start. One is the apparent evidence of Mark and Paul, who offer no obvious testimony to such a tradition; the other is the apparent evidence for the relative lateness of this tradition in Matthew and Luke, whose narratives presumably diverge so sharply precisely in the absence of a common source.[5] Granted, my putting of the case makes assumptions of its own about the history of the synoptic tradition; but although one might object that my assessment of the evidence is beholden to a particular (consensus) view of synoptic relations and dating, it should also be noted that the character of the evidence here is precisely an argument for the consensus view.

Still, Wenham finds enough in common between Matthew and Luke (both have 'an emphasis on Jesus as the Son of God, as a descendant of David, as born of Mary, having been conceived by the Holy Spirit', and both have 'a strongly Semitic flavour') to argue for common source traditions, and 'it is quite possible that they are early Palestinian traditions that Paul might well have known'.[6] (How many 'maybes' does that make so far?) Remarking on Galatians 4.4 and Romans 1.3, Wenham lists the following shared elements between the Gospel narratives and these two verses in Paul: an emphasis on Jesus as God's Son; the presumption of a natural human birth; the 'prominence' of Jesus' mother (a rather dubious inference from Paul's 'born of woman' in Galatians 4.4, it must be said); an emphasis on Davidic descent and on being born 'under the law'; and the placement of the birth of Jesus 'in an eschatological framework and within the context of Old Testament fulfilment'.[7] These points of contact, says Wenham, 'give the lie to any idea that Paul was unfamiliar with the sort of traditions about Jesus' birth that are found in the Gospels'.[8] But on the contrary, these themes (a normal birth, divine Sonship, Davidic descent, an eschatological setting) seem to me to be far too general to demand a source in common *birth* traditions.[9]

But Wenham's case is more ambitious even than this. More than just Paul's general *knowledge* of the birth traditions, he asserts that 'the birth of Jesus (and not just his death and resurrection) has theological importance for Paul'.[10] Wenham has in mind particularly belief in a virgin birth. Referring to the birth and incarnation texts quoted above, Wenham finds intimations of such a belief in that Paul only mentions Jesus' *mother*, that Jesus is called *God's* Son, and that Jesus is said to be sinless; but of themselves these indications are all held (quite rightly) to be inconclusive.[11] However, the balance is tipped for Wenham in favour of Paul's conscious affirmation of the virgin birth by Paul's choice of verb for Jesus' birth in Galatians 4.4, Romans 1.3, and Philippians 2.7: all three have *ginomai* ('become', 'come to exist'), rather than *gennaō,* the significance of which is held to be that the latter is avoided in the case of Jesus due to its association with male 'begetting'.[12] Now Wenham notes both the argument that *ginomai* in these Pauline texts emphasises entering the human state rather than birth as such (so that Jesus' *birth* is not especially in view), and the argument that *ginomai* was used synonymously with *gennaō* (so that no exceptional circumstances are needed here to explain its use in reference to Jesus' birth), and in fact Wenham plays these two arguments off against each other.[13] But it seems to me that more careful linguistic (or lexical semantic) observation clarifies the sense in which both these arguments are correct, and to the detriment of Wenham's case. The *sense* of *ginomai* in question is 'to become' or 'to come to exist'; it may *refer* to birth, and indeed where context indicates this particular point of beginning (as arguably in the case of Galatians 4.4 and Romans 1.3, but less clearly so in Philippians 2.7), the *translation* 'to be born' is appropriate (that is, 'to be born' is not a discrete sense of the verb *ginomai,* but rather the general sense 'come to exist' may be contextually modulated such that the translation equivalent 'to be born' is appropriate).[14] The net effect of these observations, then, is that Paul's usage in these texts, instead of suggesting any principled reflection on the peculiar circumstances of Jesus' birth, is such as rather to diminish any particular focus on the *birth* of Jesus as such as distinct from his 'coming to be' in the form and function in which he appeared. That is to say, rather than indicating a particular perspective on Jesus' birth, if Paul's choice of words signifies anything, it suggests a lack of specific interest in Jesus' nativity.[15] It cannot, of course, be said that Wenham's position is impossible; or rather, it might well be the case that Paul's language, as Wenham says, 'would . . . be in keeping with a belief in the Virgin Birth' – *assuming,* that is, that Paul possessed such a conviction (and even here, one notes that Matthew, who certainly did believe in the virgin birth, uses *gennaō* of Jesus, making verb use a questionable doctrinal index).[16] But to attribute such a belief to Paul on the basis of such possible associations of his language is inadequate, even irresponsible.[17]

Jesus and Paul

Our investigation of Paul and the birth of Jesus has implicated us in the broader debate over 'Jesus and Paul' (the question of the continuity and/or discontinuity of Paul with Jesus – and of the latter, or both, with traditional Christianity – one aspect of which is the dual question of Paul's knowledge of and interest in 'the Jesus of history' as opposed to 'the Christ of faith'). This debate raged at the turn of the twentieth century, and it still has the power to draw our interest a century on because of the way in which it focuses a number of far-reaching historical and theological questions.[18] In fact, Wenham's title (*Paul: Follower of Jesus or Founder of Christianity?*) harks back to that earlier period of the debate, when William Wrede (in his popularly pitched but incisive book *Paul*) notoriously dubbed Paul the 'second founder of Christianity' (who, as such, 'exercised beyond all doubt the stronger – not the better – influence').[19] And Wenham himself makes a valuable contribution to this critical issue (my brief, largely negative interaction with him on this narrower point notwithstanding).[20] Nevertheless, Wenham does not move the debate beyond its present polarisation into 'minimalist' and 'maximalist' approaches (according to one's estimate of Paul's knowledge of and interest in Jesus-tradition) – Wenham is clearly a 'maximalist', in this case attributing to Paul both a detailed knowledge of the birth traditions and a pointed christological interest in the miraculous circumstances of Jesus' birth.[21] It is a scandal to the 'maximalist' mindset that Paul should so focus on the death and resurrection as to appear to take little interest in the earthly Jesus; but the test-case of the birth of Jesus, at least, suggests just that. In that context, my own take on Paul and the birth of Jesus – Paul is wholeheartedly 'in favour of' it – is only half-joking: as the texts cited above variously testify, it is crucial for redemption that Jesus should have appeared 'in the flesh', and thus, to the degree that the birth of Jesus comes into view for Paul, it does play a positive role, at least indirectly; but the focus on redemption suggests that for Paul Jesus' identity is crucially determined by his death and resurrection (as these same texts clearly testify).

My own inclinations, then, appear to be 'minimalist' – but then I tend not to like such labels (especially as applied to *me*); and in this particular case, 'minimalist' sounds like an accusation, at least when it comes from a 'maximalist' (and the same goes the other way around, I suppose). Anyway, it is not as though I am pursuing some positive programme of 'minimalising' anything (presumably in order to deny Paul all legitimate continuity with Jesus).[22] Still, these labels do have some point, as a convenient shorthand for a substantive methodological difference. To tease this out, we can begin with a reminder that might seem to favour the 'maximalist': 'Paul' and his letters are not co-extensive – there was certainly much more to the man than we chance to find in a fragmentary collection of his occasional correspondence. Thus the 'maximalist' can always point out that to base a judgement as to Paul's knowledge of and interest in Jesus-tradition on the limited evidence of the letters is an argument from silence. But to assert, against the evidence of the letters, that Paul knew much more, and then to offer a rationale as to why this is not more in evidence (for example, Paul passed on extensive Jesus-tradition in his prior mission preaching, which he then largely assumes in his letters and typically treats allusively if at all), is, as it were, a double argument from silence.[23] One approach starts from what Paul *must* have known or supposed or been curious about (where we are certain of the reality of something that, unfortunately, lies largely hidden from view), while the other approach observes as its limits what we are *justified* in asserting about Paul. For one, the fragments of Jesus material in Paul are like the tip of an iceberg, from which a much larger mass may be inferred, while for the other, they are like pieces of an ancient mosaic that may be re-assembled only in relation to one other (but not as part of a larger scene, unless such is discovered in direct connection). For the former approach, the 'mights', 'maybes', 'possiblys' and 'quite likelys' multiply; and assertions of what *might* be the case often feel like a plea for what *needs to be the case*. Yes, indeed, Paul *may* have known the Christmas story and the doctrine of the virgin birth; but we should all agree that we need more on which to base such a claim than just our fondness for the thought. To adapt a hard-nosed historical axiom: If you can't show it, you don't know it.[24]

On letting Paul be himself

So where have we come to on Paul and the birth of Jesus? We have brought to attention a handful of relevant verses in Paul: in particular, three that depict Jesus' appearance more globally (Rom. 8.3; 2 Cor. 5.21; 8.9) and three that (arguably) make some reference to Jesus' birth (Gal. 4.4; Rom. 1.3; Phil. 2.7). However, our initial impression was that, even where Jesus' birth is somewhat in view, the emphasis does not lie there – certainly, there is not enough here to speak of theological reflection specifically on the *birth* of Jesus. We then examined a recent claim to the contrary. But that claim has been found wanting. So why bother with Paul at all? Are the results only negative?

Well, I would argue, to begin with, that 'negative' results can themselves be of positive benefit. Paul is an important early historical and theological witness, so we could hardly avoid attending to his testimony; and certain specific claims that have recently been made for the Pauline evidence are surely worth investigating. If nothing else, a negative result here might help us face soberly the apparent lateness and divergence of the birth narratives, and the significance of this for the doctrine of the virgin birth associated with them (while such earlier sources as there might have been remain for us shrouded in darkness – which may not be ultimately satisfying, but if that is where we are, it is good to know where we stand). Here, a sense of proportion is called for. It has long been noted how early twentieth-century 'fundamentalist' reactions to modern 'liberal' questioning of the doctrine of the virgin birth made it 'the crucial test of Christian belief', and thus 'elevated it . . . to a position of importance it probably never had before'.[25] As one contemporary theologian

has put it, 'the virginal conception is not a touchstone of
Christian orthodoxy or a dogma to be believed on pain of damna-
tion (again, such thinking implies a later belief system that
supplants biblical faith)'; rather, it is 'a sign of faith for the faithful, speaking to many (admittedly not to all) believers of what is
signified by this sign, namely the full presence of God in the full
story of Jesus'.[26]

But actually, I would want to raise the case of Paul's unique
perspective without assigning a value to it as such – here it is of
particular value that Paul should be allowed to stand out as
different, and not be assimilated into subsequent expectations or
made subject to the strictures of an anachronistic sense of propriety.
For Paul does indeed have a 'story of Jesus', as recent 'narrative'
readings of Paul have emphasised.[27] It is instructive to see how
differently Paul focuses that story from what we might have
expected, versed as we are in the Gospel stories – how he
(notoriously) views the whole so overwhelmingly through the death
and resurrection of Jesus. Wrede's unflinching ability to let Paul
be Paul – as he put it, 'it is harder to interpret Paul's doctrine to
one who half understands him than to one who knows nothing
about him' – is a large part of the abiding value of his often
provocative work (no matter how much it might now stand in
need of correction).[28] 'What *we* prize in the man Jesus plays no
part whatever in the thought of the apostle. Nothing is further
aloof from him than religious veneration for a hero.'[29]

> [W]hat was most important to him in the humanity of Jesus
> was not the ethical and religious value of his person or his earthly
> life, but his abnegation of his divine existence. In the actual 'life'
> of Jesus – we exclude the assumption of humanity and the
> resurrection – only one event is important to Paul, namely the
> destruction of that life, Jesus' death. But again this is not, in his
> eyes, the moral act of a man – he is as far as possible from martyr-
> worship in this sense . . .[30]

'To reproach Paul is idle. He did not put a religion together by
mere caprice, but was guided by internal and external necessity.

[But] if we do not wish to deprive both figures of all historical distinctness, the name "disciple of Jesus" has little applicability to Paul, if it is used to denote an historical relation.'[31] 'Paul's whole innovation is comprised in this, that he laid the foundation of religion . . . in the incarnation, death and resurrection of Christ. If we are to designate the character of this conception we cannot avoid the word "myth".'[32] If Wrede's account poses a challenge to traditional assumptions – indeed, a challenge that could not go unanswered – it is worth pondering what distorting effects some forms of *defence* of Paul might have.[33]

So, quite apart from theological comparisons between Paul and the Gospel narratives, these Pauline texts develop theological interests of their own: for instance, Paul shows himself to be concerned not so much with Jesus' nativity as with that of his followers, or rather, their 'adoption' as 'children of God' in Christ, God's Son (a theme that enters significantly into both the Galatians 4 and Romans 8 texts, and into Romans 1.3 via 2 Samuel 7).[34] With Paul, we have to imagine ourselves back to a point where Christmas is still very much in the shadow of Easter – perhaps before the Christmas story had come into view at all. If indeed Christian theology was alive and well in its beginnings with Paul without principled reflection on the birth of Jesus – if the faith was nourished for a time without that part of the story – that gives perspective to our own different standpoint (and it heightens the irony of a cultural situation where for many the last remaining personal attachment to the story of Jesus is in the annual celebration of Christmas).[35] But we should not smuggle in here the assumption that Paul's standpoint is the essential one. Just because Paul does not theologise about Jesus' birth, that does not of itself make it an unworthy subject for theological reflection. While again not wishing to put a value on it, we could regard Paul's point of view as being limited (and limiting) in certain important respects. Contemporary theology might wish to connect Jesus' death not so much with the resurrection (as conceived by Paul) as with an exemplary *life* of obedience, beginning in human birth, and culminating in a martyr's death – and here, Gospel and canon have preceded us (and it has been suggested that Paul himself was no stranger to such christological themes).[36]

So Paul must be allowed to be Paul. As a final suggestion, then, of how different things might now look by his lights, I offer this speculation: if we had it Paul's way we would not even have met in Manchester to mark the millennium with a Symposium on 'the birth of Jesus'. For our subject, of course, would have to be 'the death and resurrection of Jesus'. And we would not meet until another thirty years or so, for surely Paul would not have oriented the calendar from the birth of a historic personage, as it were, but from the rebirth of all creation in Christ's dying and rising again. This is an intriguing possibility to contemplate, not least in respect to the question of how well Paul's perspective will seem to us to have worn, after two thousand years, in that imagined parallel universe.

Suggested further reading

VICTOR PAUL FURNISH, *Jesus According to Paul* (Understanding Jesus Today; Cambridge: Cambridge University Press, 1993).

LUKE TIMOTHY JOHNSON, *Living Jesus: Learning the Heart of the Gospel* (New York: HarperSanFrancisco, 1999).

MARINUS DE JONGE, *God's Final Envoy: Early Christology and Jesus' Own View of His Mission* (Grand Rapids: Eerdmans, 1998).

DAVID WENHAM, *Paul: Follower of Jesus or Founder of Christianity?* (Grand Rapids: Eerdmans, 1995).

WILLIAM WREDE, *Paul* (trans. E. Lummis; London: Philip Green, 1907).

CHAPTER FIVE

DNA OF OUR DNA

Arthur Peacocke

Introduction

The birth narratives in the early chapters of the Gospels of Matthew and Luke (Matt. 1.18–2.12; Luke 1.26–56 and 2.1–20) have provided the principal basis for the belief that Jesus was born of his mother Mary without the agency of a human father, that is by the direct action of God (as 'the Holy Spirit'); and that she was later married to Joseph. It has also been inferred as congruent with, and a deduction from, the affirmation of Jesus as being both 'God and man', that is the doctrine of the incarnation in its most explicitly ontological form. However, according to the Roman Catholic scholar Raymond E. Brown, 'Both Protestant and Catholic theologians have stated clearly that the bodily fatherhood of Joseph would not have excluded the fatherhood of God'[1] and quotes the 'relatively conservative' Catholic theologian, J. Ratzinger: 'According to the faith of the Church the Sonship of Jesus does not rest on the fact that Jesus had no human father: the doctrine of Jesus' divinity would not be affected if Jesus had been the product of a normal marriage. For the Sonship of which faith speaks is not a biological but an ontological fact, an event not in time but in God's eternity.'[2] The two Gospel narratives have been intensively studied in relation to their historicity and to this we shall have to revert. Before doing so, it is pertinent to stress the issues raised by so-called 'miracles' in general and, in particular,

by our scientific knowledge in relation to the very notion of a
'virginal conception' of Jesus – commonly called the virgin birth,
although it is really the nature of Jesus' beginning as a living being
that is involved. It is with respect to this that modern biological
science poses some hard questions.

Miracle and the scientific view of the world

We are, of course, free to use the word miracle in whatever way
suits us in the present intellectual climate and it has, in fact,
undergone much redefinition in the course of time. In a *biblical*
concordance it will often be pointed out that the English word
miracle etymologically translates words standing for 'wonder', 'an
act of power' or 'a sign'. Nevertheless, since the general estab-
lishment of the non-biblical idea of an 'order' of nature, ordinary
usage of the word implies 'some contrast with the natural order'
and an event 'not fully explicable by naturalistic means'.[3] Indeed
the *Shorter Oxford English Dictionary* gives as its principal meaning:
'A marvellous event exceeding the known powers of nature, and
therefore supposed to be due to the special intervention of the
Deity or of some supernatural agency.' It is in this sense that the
virginal conception of Jesus is usually taken to be a miracle that
initiates his human life.

Clearly there are general considerations which weigh heavily
against the occurrence of such events at all:

- our increasing ability in the last three hundred years to
  account for the general sequence of regular events in terms
  of a closed causal nexus;

- the recognition that one of the principal grounds for affirm-
  ing the existence of God as Creator, who is other than the
  observed world (including the human one) and is both
  the source of the very existence of that world and of its
  inbuilt rationality, is the scientific account of the causal
  nexus;

- and the requirement that historical evidence for such events to be convincing has to be proportionally greater the more unusual the event, the more it is said to rupture known regularities – especially in the form of well-established scientific 'laws of nature'.

In the case of the alleged virginal conception of Jesus, there are further particular considerations that are relevant:

- it scarcely needs the warrant of science, ancient or modern, to affirm that the birth of a human baby normally requires intercourse between a man and a woman (even when, as the errant servant girl said to her mistress, on the birth of her unannounced baby, 'It's only a very little one'!);
- the ancient belief that the female human being is a mere receptacle for the new life which comes entirely from the male is false, for in the last one hundred and fifty years or so biological science has firmly established that the human embryo begins with the entry into a female ovum of a male sperm;
- hence, the historical evidence that a woman has, after the usual nine months gestation, had a baby without having been the recipient of a male sperm would have to be exceedingly strong – and it is notoriously very weak indeed in the case of Jesus' mother.

For even the cautious Raymond Brown has concluded that 'the *scientifically controllable* biblical evidence leaves the question of the historicity of the virginal conception unresolved'.[4] By 'scientifically controllable biblical evidence' he quite properly means 'evidence constituted by tradition from identifiable witnesses of the events involved, when that tradition is traceably preserved and not in conflict with other traditions'.[5] Brown's verdict of 'unresolved' would be regarded as overcautious by other scholars less restrained by traditional dogma. Thus John Macquarrie, an Anglican, affirms that '. . . our historical information is negligible . . . apart from . . . scraps of doubtful information, the birth narratives [of Matthew and Luke] are manifestly legendary in character'.[6] And C. J. Cadoux, a Congregationalist, concluded his discussion of the matter thus:

> Nor indeed is it enough for scholars to leave the issue [of the virginal conception] open, on the sole ground that the evidence for the miraculous birth is insufficient. If a miracle is asserted to have occurred, and cogent evidence for its occurrence cannot be adduced, and belief in it can be readily accounted for along other lines, the duty of scholars is not to leave the reality of it an open question, but to reject it, not as inconceivable, but as in all probability not true.[7]

There are, moreover, further developments in our knowledge of human nature which cannot but affect our judgement in this matter:

- that, in accordance actually with the prevailing biblical understanding, human beings are psychosomatic unities – not made up of two or three distinct entities (body/mind/soul) but constituted of whatever the physicists find basic (atoms, or, below them, quarks or whatever) with real emergent mental and (I would add) spiritual capacities;

- human beings are now realised to be much more under the leash of their genetic endowment than previously thought – not controlled or directed but constrained by it.

The virginal conception and biology

This is the background to considering other hard questions concerning the virginal conception which biology poses for us today. The relevant facts, determined by the biology of the last one hundred and fifty years, are as follows. Any complete human being begins life by the union of an ovum from a female human being and a spermatozoon from a male one. The sex of the fertilised ovum, and so of the baby that is born, is determined by a particular pair of chromosomes present in all the ordinary (somatic) cells of human beings – those in females being both of the same type denoted as X (so XX), and those in males being different, one X and the other of type Y (so XY). These pairs of chromosomes carry in their DNA genes for various characteristics, as do the other twenty-two pairs of chromosomes in somatic cells that do not differ in kind from male to female. In the formation of ova and spermatozoa these ordinary, somatic cells split so that the members of the various pairs of chromosomes separate out into new half-cells (an ovum or a sperm cell) containing one chromosome only of each of those pairs. Human conception begins with the union of two such 'half-cells' one from each parent. The ovum from the mother *always* contributes an X-type chromosome to this new line of cells while the father contributes *either* an X *or* a Y: if the former, a female combined cell (XX) results; if the latter, a male one (XY) – with a 50:50 chance. This is how all human beings begin and this is how the sex of the resulting child is determined from its beginning. Furthermore, if no male is involved, as in insect parthenogenesis, the offspring are female, because no Y chromosomes are available. It is no use calling upon cases of *natural* parthenogenesis to support the virginal conception of a *male* Jesus!

For Mary to have been pregnant with the foetus that became Jesus without the involvement of a human father – that is, without a Y chromosome coming from (say) Joseph – there are, biologically only two possibilities. Either (1) Mary provided the ovum which was then transformed by an act of God (impregnation by the Holy Spirit?) into a viable, reproducing cell, as if a sperm had entered the ovum; or (2) there was created such an impregnated ovum within her uterus with no contribution from Mary's own genetic heritage at all. As Canon Derek Stanesby has put it, in a trenchant analysis of what the virginal conception really implies: 'Biologically, either Mary provided the ovum for impregnation by the Holy Ghost and so contributed to her son's genetic inheritance, or she was simply a vessel containing and nourishing the divinely implanted seed, that is, a surrogate mother.'[8]

According to the first possibility for a virginal conception (1), Mary would have contributed an X chromosome to the cells of Jesus but, for Jesus to be male, the Y chromosome (not coming from a human father) would have had to have been created *de novo* by God. The X (and other) chromosomes in Jesus' cells would have had, through Mary's genetic predecessors, a particular inheritance as a member of the evolved species *homo sapiens*. But, we cannot avoid asking, what genetic characteristics would be created in Jesus' Y (and other) chromosomes, normally derived from the sperm of a human father? The genetic constitution of a human being is foundational to their humanity and so of their personhood. So, in case (1), really to have been human, Jesus would have had to have been provided with an intact created set of human genes, on the Y and other chromosomes. What genetic information was encoded in these miraculously created genes? Did God give him a set to make his characteristics (shape of nose, colour of hair, blood group, etc.) mimic what Joseph *would* have provided had he been involved, or what? Implausible though this all sounds, this possibility at least has the merit of retaining a link of Jesus with humanity through the genetic contribution of Mary.

But even that is precluded by the possibility (2), mooted above, in which Mary is simply a vessel in which is implanted an already fertilised ovum – indeed a kind of surrogate mother. In this case (2), Jesus' entire genetic constitution (carried on the X and Y and all the other chromosomes) would have had to have been created *de novo*. So the question arises *a fortiori*, what genes did God choose to put in the cells from which the embryo of Jesus developed during what is implied, in the two Gospel accounts, to be a normal gestation period? *Could* Jesus then be said to be genuinely human at all if this was his miraculous origin? Or was he just a *copy* of a human being but with all his genetic endowment, and so bodily features, not actually continuous with our evolved nature at all?

To pile Ossia on Pelion, one improbability on another, one has further to recognise what is actually being proposed in either form of the virginal conception in the light of the knowledge we now have of the processes of life. This belief means that God must suddenly have brought into existence either (1) a complete spermatazoon, which then entered an ovum of Mary, or (2) a completely fertilised ovum, since all the reports assume the usual nine-month gestation period needed for the multicellular embryo to develop to be ready for birth. Each of these biological entities, especially the second, is an enormously complex system of thousands of atoms in actual molecules, some very large such as DNA, engaged in dynamic biological activity in an organisation more complex than that of any modern factory! This really would be a wonder-working magical kind of act – a 'special creation' *de novo* of exactly the type the so-called 'creationists' argue for – an act producing an entity resembling a human being but not actually sharing in our evolved humanity.

Thus the present understanding of the biology of reproduction and of heredity reveals the doctrine of the virginal conception to be postulating an extraordinary, almost magical, divine act of suddenly bringing into existence a complex biological entity. All the evidence is that is *not* how God has created and is creating – certainly not the God whose mode of being and becoming it is possible to believe in today.

Biology and doctrine

In the light of our biological knowledge it is then impossible to see how Jesus could be said to share our human nature, if he came into existence by a virginal conception of the kind traditionally proposed. This means that the doctrine of the virginal conception is also *theologically* inadequate if Jesus is to be relevant to our human destiny. As Stanesby says,

> In summary, a divine set of genes nurtured by a surrogate mother would hardly result in the Incarnate Lord of the Christian faith. If the world, including man, has an evolutionary history, then incarnation (for salvation) must involve identification with, not dissociation from, that history.[9]

John Macquarrie has expressed the point thus:

> . . . if we suppose Christ to have been conceived and born in an
> altogether unique way, then it seems that we have separated him
> from the rest of the human race and thereby made him irrelevant
> to the human quest for salvation or for the true life. We would
> be saying not that he is the revelation of God shedding light on
> our darkness, but that he is an altogether unintelligible anomaly,
> thrust into the middle of history.[10]

Indeed it is now, in the light of the science I have been indicating,
actually inconsistent with the doctrine of the incarnation which
insists that it is a *complete* human nature that is united with God
(as *Logos*, or as 'God the Son'). Jesus must be bone of our bone,
flesh of our flesh and DNA of our DNA, DNA from a human
father, in order to have any salvific role for humanity. For, as
Gregory of Nazianzus has famously said, 'what he has not assumed
he has not healed'.[11]

Furthermore, these scientifically-based considerations also now
show, in a way which was less obvious before they could be brought
to bear on the question, that theologically speaking the doctrine
of the virginal conception is actually 'docetic'[12] in its implications.[13]
For if Jesus' humanity *was* only apparent, in the biological sense
described above, and so not real (indeed artificial, not natural)
and if Jesus was, in some way, also divine, then he would indeed
have been 'a divine being . . . dressed up as a man in order to
communicate revelations', which is the core of the definition of
the heresy of docetism.

Conclusion

Briefly, for Jesus to be fully human he had, for both biological
and theological reasons, to have a human father as well as a human
mother and the weight of the historical evidence strongly indicates
that this was so – and that it was probably Joseph. Any theology
for a scientific age which is concerned with the significance of
Jesus of Nazareth now has to start at this point.

Suggested further reading

RAYMOND E. BROWN, *The Virginal Conception and Bodily Resurrection of Jesus* (New York: Paulist Press, 1973).

——, *The Birth of the Messiah* (London: Geoffrey Chapman and Garden City, New York: Doubleday, 1977).

HUGH MONTEFIORE, *The Womb and the Tomb: The Mystery of the Birth and Resurrection of Jesus* (London: Fount Paperbacks, HarperCollins, 1992).

III

JESUS:
MORE THAN THE FULL STORY

CHAPTER SIX

THE VALUE OF BEING VIRGINAL: MARY AND ANNA IN THE LUKAN INFANCY PROLOGUE

Todd Klutz

Echoes of Scripture in the discourse of misogyny

The religious and aesthetic tradition to which most of our images of the birth of Jesus belong is anything but univocal about women. Ambivalence about the feminine, and thus about matters of gender in general, can be detected in Christian sources not only by comparing multiple works of art or literature – say Johannes Vermeer's *Allegory of Faith* (*c.* 1671–4) with Carlo Crivelli's *The Annunciation, with Saint Emidius* (1486) – but also by analysing the discursive strategies of a single Christian image or text. As illustrated below, a particularly rich instance of ideological polyphony regarding women is realised in the representation of chaste women in the two-volume work increasingly known as 'Luke–Acts'. Before the key units of discourse on this topic in the Lukan writings are subjected to critical scrutiny, however, and in order to appreciate some of the ways early Christian ambivalence in this area may have contributed to gender troubles in more recent times, at least brief attention will be given to two nineteenth-century philosophical discourses about women.

The pessimist Arthur Schopenhauer (1788–1860), in arguing that women 'as a whole, are and remain thorough and incurable philistines',[1] calls on the past for support. 'The peoples of antiquity', Schopenhauer observes, 'have recognised what is the proper position of women far better than we have, we with our Old

French gallantry and insipid women-veneration, that highest flower of Christian-Germanic stupidity which has served only to make women so rude and arrogant that one is . . . reminded of the sacred apes of Benares which, conscious of their own sanctity and inviolability, thought themselves at liberty to do whatever they pleased.'² The palpable misogyny exemplified in this passage, for which Schopenhauer is deservedly infamous, is not without parallel in the writings of Friedrich Nietzsche (1844–1900), who, it should not be overlooked, had carefully read Schopenhauer and, though scarcely his disciple in any narrow sense of the word, shared his conviction that Europe's exaltation of the feminine was alien to the spirit of earlier and stronger societies.³ Notwithstanding their agreement on this matter, however, and in arguing that efforts in his own time to enlighten women and give them independence constituted 'one of the worst developments in the general uglification of Europe',⁴ Nietzsche makes a strikingly favourable reference to 'the Church' that contrasts sharply with Schopenhauer's bitter castigation of 'Christian-Germanic stupidity': 'We men', Nietzsche declares, 'want woman to cease compromising herself through enlightenment: just as it was man's care and consideration for woman which led the Church to decree: *mulier taceat in ecclesia*!'⁵ Thus, while both thinkers are implicated in the discursive practices of nineteenth-century German male hegemony, their respective perceptions of what role Christian institutions had played in shaping the conditions of European women in their own times are substantially different.

For purposes of the present essay what is most arresting about the two passages cited above is the presence in each of echoes of the New Testament. Nietzsche's use of the Latin clause 'mulier taceat in ecclesia' is the most obvious case in point. Although it does not correspond precisely to the Vulgate of either 1 Corinthians 14.34 ('mulieres in ecclesiis taceant') or 1 Timothy 2.11 ('mulier in silentio discat'), its recollection of the agonistic situations to which 1 Corinthians and the Pastoral Epistles were originally addressed highlights some of the earliest antecedents of the tension noted above between Schopenhauer and Nietzsche; namely, and as many commentators on 1 Corinthians and the Pastoral Epistles have rightly observed, the authors of these documents themselves and their audiences held diverse and sometimes conflicting views on what modes of conduct were most appropriate for female members of the churches.[6]

The echoes of Pauline and Deutero-Pauline material in the extract from Nietzsche are far more straightforward than any biblical overtones discernible in Schopenhauer's piece. The latter, in fact, is easy to read – even for New Testament scholars who are predisposed to find (or create) intertextual resonances in everything they interpret – as conveying no echo whatsoever of the New Testament, however diffractive or indirect. Yet, if recent theories of language that view all discourse as moulded by social conflict and ideological struggle are right, interpretations that are 'easy' and monologic will normally be wrong. In this light Schopenhauer's juxtaposition of German society's alleged 'Old French gallantry' and 'insipid women-veneration' almost certainly merits further inspection, particularly since the cultural history which this juxtaposition evokes provides a hermeneutical bridge between the interpretative present and the alien past that shaped the New Testament passages treated below.

A note of caution, however, should be issued at the outset of this inquiry. On the one hand, and as Simone de Beauvoir has argued in far greater detail than can be offered here, it would be misleading to assert any simple continuity between the 'women-veneration' that Schopenhauer associates with France and the various forms of feminism that now exist in most parts of the western world.[7] But on the other hand, and as de Beauvoir appreciates much too feebly, male domination of women in nineteenth-century Europe varied considerably in degree from one society to the next, with progressive attitudes towards women having encountered much stiffer resistance in Germany than in France;[8] moreover, as nearly all ambivalence among German liberals toward French political ideas was swept away by the widespread hostility provoked by France's aggressive foreign policy in 1840[9] – eleven years before the publication of Schopenhauer's

Parerga and Paralipomena – Schopenhauer's insinuation that his German contemporaries had become disgustingly drunk on the wine of Gallican decadence is difficult to construe as anything other than the hyperbolic rhetoric of a scapegoating and misogynist imagination.

To repudiate Schopenhauer's claim that German society had been deeply penetrated by French liberalism, however, is not to contest the underlying assumption that Germany was, in general, more androcentric than France was at this time. Indeed, according to historian Gordon R. Craig, Germany's 'ruling class was as intent upon keeping the female population in a state of dependence as it was upon combatting socialism'.[10] Craig continues:

> All the expedients of the law, every form of financial and moral pressure, were employed to maintain male dominance in state, society, and the home. Women were denied basic civil rights (they could not vote and in most states were barred from membership in political organizations and trade unions) and were excluded from both any share in the governance of the country and employment in any of its administrative agencies.[11]

Furthermore, and as Craig goes on to observe, the predicament of German women in the nineteenth century looks even more deplorable when compared with the experience of their female contemporaries in many other parts of Europe – especially France, where women had much greater freedom to participate in the public life of their country.[12]

Why French women in particular fared better than their counterparts in Germany is a large and complex subject that lies outside the topical frame of the present inquiry. Nevertheless, at least one aspect of this question deserves to be mentioned here, namely the role of the Virgin Mary in shaping the identities of women in the last twenty centuries, especially (but not exclusively) in countries like France where Catholic assumptions and values are famous for inventing ways to endure long after the publication of their obituaries. In this connection, of course, the Marian legacy is itself scarcely univocal; yet, in regard to European attitudes in the nineteenth century, it needs to be remembered that the only real alternative to ambivalence about the feminine was aversion to it. Thus, if Jaroslav Pelikan is correct to rate Mary 'the woman *par excellence* for most of western history'[13] and to estimate the subtleties of her imagery as central to how the feminine in general has been perceived in the same cultural narrative, Mary could not have failed to contribute – in one complex way or another – to the contrast noted above. The aim of the discussion below, then, is to show that the same kinds of subtleties which made this contribution possible can also be detected in Luke–Acts, especially in the characterisation of Mary, but also in the portrayal of other female characters to whom special chastity is attributed.

The dangerous allure of female chastity in Luke–Acts

In New Testament scholarship of the present century, Luke–Acts has often been attributed a theological point of view which is more like that of the Pastoral Epistles than like that of the undisputed writings of Paul.[14] In at least some cases, moreover, this interpretation has arisen from a combination of almost naive devotion to the theology of the so-called 'real Paul' on the one hand and overconfident assumptions about what exactly this theology consists of on the other. An especially interesting example of this tendency is found in Ernst Haenchen's influential commentary on the Acts of the Apostles, which, despite its enduring reputation as a model of historical method, exemplifies a subtle but surprising form of piety in its effort to distance the author of Acts as far as possible from Paul.

Having argued that the author of Acts was no true collaborator of Paul but rather one who viewed the great missionary 'through the eyes of a later age',[15] Haenchen concludes his discussion of this matter on a peculiar and suspiciously theological note: 'We need have no qualms about letting this truth [i.e. that Luke knew very little about "the real Paul"] be the last word,' he stresses, 'for without detracting from Luke's real merit, it ensures that *the gospel according to Paul will not be robbed of its due*' (italics mine).[16] Now

precisely what the gospel according to Paul is '*due*', particularly in
the context of a supposedly historical and critical commentary on
Acts, is by no means clear; in this regard the best conjecture that
can be entertained here is that, at least in Haenchen's eyes, the
Pauline message still possesses enough cultural capital to attract
attention from theological thieves, many of whose dubious devices
have been moulded by the unreliable narrator of Acts. But more
significant for the present investigation, at no point in Haenchen's
treatment of Paul's relationship with Luke are the two writers'
respective representations of and attitudes toward women analysed
or compared. Had Haenchen undertaken this task, as indeed he
is given fair opportunity to do by the reference in Acts 21.9 to the
evangelist Philip's 'four virgin daughters who prophesied', his
treatment of Luke's relation to Paul may well have been substantially different from what it is; for on no issue is the perspective
of Acts closer to that of the undisputed Pauline writings, or more
distant from that of the Pastoral letters, than on the subject of
women.[17]

By itself and on the surface, the reference noted above to Philip's
daughters is not particularly noteworthy. Indeed, one of the most
striking aspects of the daughters' portrayal is that, immediately
after this single reference to them, they disappear from Luke's
narrative, never to appear in it again. Furthermore, and against
anyone disposed to see in the daughters' prophetic function an
egalitarian stance towards women on the part of Luke, the narrator
of this episode (Acts 21.1–14) never actually cites any prophetic
utterance which these four figures might be imagined to have
produced; to make matters worse, in the immediately ensuing co-
text the narrator does cite the inspired speech of the Judaean
prophet Agabus (Acts 21.10–11), who, in addition to predicting
that Paul will be bound by the Jews of Jerusalem and handed over
to the Gentiles, is male. And finally, like the vast majority of women
mentioned in ancient literature, the four women of Acts 21.9 are
introduced and defined in terms of their relation to a significant
male other, namely their father, Philip the evangelist, to whose
honour, moreover, their prophetic gifts indirectly contribute.

However, when viewed in relation to the rest of its Lukan co-text, this brief reference takes on an additional layer of significance and interest. More specifically, and as Turid K. Seim has recently pointed out, when the characterisation of Philip's daughters is compared with that of other women in Luke–Acts to whom prophetic powers are attributed, a remarkable pattern emerges: namely, of the seven women who fit this description (Elizabeth, Mary, Anna and Philip's daughters), six are portrayed as either virginal or notably chaste in some other way.[18] The general effect of this pattern is to suggest that at least as far as the author of Luke–Acts was concerned, sexual innocence and other forms of chastity could function in certain types of contexts – for women no less than for men – both as a positive alternative to the conventional routines of marriage and childbearing and as a strategy for acquiring prophetic power and its attendant status.

Significantly, the perspective just summarised was neither inevitable nor understood to be natural in Luke's cultural context. This can be seen with the aid of one simple comparative exercise pertaining to the age(s) of Philip's daughters. Although the narrator of Acts 21.1–14 gives no explicit information regarding the age of any of these four women, he does leave a few clues that allow some rough but helpful guesses to be made. Most important, as the daughters are implied to be living in the home of their father (Acts 21.8–9), who neither here nor in Luke's previous references to him (e.g. Acts 6.1–6; 8.4–40) is ever characterised as elderly, all four of them should almost certainly be seen as relatively young women, falling somewhere between the earliest age at which they might be given in marriage (i.e. around twelve and a half) to say forty years old. This profile receives additional support from the narrator's observation that the daughters were 'virgins' – a characterisation that would have been meaningless had they been understood to be too young for marriage and its procreative activities – and from the absence of any hint that they might have been elderly, a feature that distinguishes them for instance from the prophetess Anna, who in Luke's words was 'of a great age' (Luke 2.36).

Now the wider significance of these observations becomes evident only when they are viewed in light of select teachings found in the Pastoral letters – especially 1 Timothy and Titus – regarding marriage and proper modes of conduct for the churches' women. In 1 Timothy 2.15, for instance, the eternal salvation of women is conceptualised as contingent on their fulfilment of the conventional female roles of child-bearer and wife,[19] conditions which Philip's daughters, notwithstanding their positive image in Acts, could not claim to have fulfilled. Consistent with the teaching of 1 Timothy 2.15, moreover, and in contrast with the Lukan images outlined above, the Pastorals include no images or paraenetic material that could promote celibacy as an alternative to marriage and the conventional family; on the contrary, renunciation of marriage and other forms of asceticism are labelled as demonically inspired forms of deviance (1 Tim. 4.1–5), while marriage and family life are not only assumed to be normative (1 Tim. 2.15; 3:2–5; Titus 2.3–5) but also explicitly affirmed and given positive value (1 Tim. 5.11–14).

Almost certainly, one of the main motives behind this affirmation of traditional norms and household hierarchies was to protect the churches' fragile reputation against public criticism from people outside the Christian community (1 Tim. 3.7; 5.14; Titus 2.5, 8).[20] Yet the price paid by women for this strategy should not be overlooked; namely, none of the unconventional options made available to them by Luke, as earlier by Paul (e.g. 1 Cor. 7.8, 20, 24), remains open.

These observations provide good soil for a potentially fruitful discussion of Anna, who is portrayed in Luke 2.36–38 as a witness to the infant Jesus. Unlike the daughters of Philip, for instance, Anna is depicted as advanced in age and, though having lived for the greatest portion of her life as a widow, as having once been married. On the other hand, though, and just as important, Anna certainly does resemble Philip's daughters, in ways that are very important for the present analysis. For instance, while the term used in Luke 2.36 to denote Anna as a 'prophetess' (the feminine noun *prophētis*) differs in form from that used in Acts 21.9 with reference to the prophesying daughters of Philip (a participle from the verb *prophēteuō*), the two words belong to the same lexical group and serve very similar narrative functions in these two contexts. Furthermore, although the period of Anna's virginity is implied to have ceased during her relatively brief marriage, the explicit reference to her premarital state of virginity (*partheneia*) and the assertion that her life as a widow was distinguished by a continuous display of ascetic devotion combine to create an image of a woman whose long subjugation of sexual passion is, if anything, even more impressive than that of the young virgins of Acts 21.9.

Once again the key features of the Lukan narrative acquire additional force when compared with select facets of the Pastoral letters. Most notably, in 1 Timothy 5.9–16, the teaching of which has sometimes been seen as nicely illustrated by Luke's portrayal of Anna, advice is given concerning women who have become widows during their youth. The passage, it should be acknowledged, contains a handful of discursive tensions and ambiguities. Yet its ultimate force for this particular class of widows – its main illocutionary goal – becomes crystalline by the unit's end: in order to prevent themselves from evolving into 'gossips and busybodies' (1 Tim. 5.13), and so as to deny 'the adversary' any occasion to slander the churches (1 Tim. 5.14), these women must be urged to 'marry, bear children' and devote themselves to proper management of their own households.

Strikingly, therefore, by not having remarried after becoming a widow in her youth, Anna deviates from the prescriptions given in 1 Timothy 5.14.[21] And, in light of the same letter's effort to place strict limitations on the speech of women in the churches' worship meetings (1 Tim. 2.11–12), Anna's prophetic role in Luke 2.36–38 should perhaps be understood as an example of precisely the sort of thing which the author of the Pastorals is emphatically trying to discourage. Thus, as with the daughters of Philip so with Anna, the author of Luke–Acts deserves to be seen as an advocate of behavioural options which neither conform to conventional norms nor display anxiety about the possibility of public criticism.

None of these observations about Anna and the daughters of Philip are irrelevant to the interpretation of Luke's depiction of Mary the mother of Jesus. For instance, although neither the Greek noun normally translated 'virgin' (*parthenos*) in Luke 1.27 nor the echoes of LXX Isaiah 7.14 in the same context absolutely require Mary to be seen as anything more than a young unmarried woman, the use of the same term in Acts 21.9, and of a noun from the same etymological group in Luke 2.36 (*partheneia*), to convey clear and specific overtones of sexual innocence virtually requires similar connotations to be inferred from Luke's initial references to Mary.[22]

In this light, moreover, and once again with Luke's images of Anna and the daughters of Philip firmly in mind, the prominence of 'the Holy Spirit' in this same context – a motif that is both placed in the foreground and explained via the angel Gabriel's use of synthetic parallelism ('The Holy Spirit will come upon you, and the power of the Most High will overshadow you'; Luke 1.35) – reinforces the observation made above concerning the relationship between chastity and the Spirit of prophecy; namely, in Luke's view the former appears to have functioned as a condition, in at least some instances, for experience of the latter. Accordingly, readers should not be surprised when, subsequently, Mary the virgin is cited as speaking in a manner that not only manifests rich patterns of biblical intertextuality and parallelism (e.g. Luke 1.51b–54a), but also shows signs of prophetic inspiration and authority.[23]

Two other details in Luke's representation of Mary serve especially well to strengthen this same remarkably favourable portrayal. First of all, in what is undoubtedly a deliberately conceived contrast to Zechariah, who is negatively described by Gabriel as having lacked faith and as therefore having suffered a temporary curse on his organs of speech (Luke 1.19–20), Mary is implied by the same angel to possess unique favour with the God of Israel (Luke 1.28, 30), and shortly thereafter is repeatedly honoured by Zechariah's wife Elizabeth (Luke 1.41–45) – once, in Luke 1.45, in connection with Mary's possession of precisely that virtue which Zechariah earlier is said to have lacked, namely faith in the word of the Lord (Luke 1.20, 45).

And finally, in the dialogue of Mary and Elizabeth in Luke 1.39–56, the uniquely positive status of Mary is suggested by far more than the impressive style of her own hymn of praise. For as soon as the women's speeches are compared, particularly in terms of tenor (i.e. the interpersonal aspects of register), an arresting asymmetry becomes apparent; to be more precise, whereas Elizabeth brings into the foreground her desire to bestow honour on Mary – she begins and ends her discourse by describing Mary as 'blessed' (Luke 1.42, 45), both she and her own unborn son underscore the greatness of the child to be born to Mary (Luke 1.41–42, 44), and she calls Mary 'the mother of my Lord' (Luke 1.43) – Mary shows no sign of sensing any obligation to recipro-cate her relative's gifts of honour. On the contrary, rather than ascribe any special merit to Elizabeth, Mary directs all her praise to her Lord, highlighting the deity's mighty agency in a vibratory sequence of salvific reversals (Luke 1.52–53), but notably without making even one unambiguous reference to her kinswoman.

Like the favourable features in Luke's characterisations of Anna and the daughters of Philip, the details summarised above from the Lukan representation of Mary do not merely contribute to positive images of particular female actors on the stage of his narrative, but ultimately beckon certain types of female hearers in the implied audience to a life of spiritual adventure, to a socio-religious experiment of fashioning themselves in accordance with unconventional modes of existence and action that were anything but uncontroversial in Luke's cultural milieu. Furthermore, inasmuch as some of these images occur in sections of Luke's Gospel that are not parallelled in Matthew (Luke 1:26–38, 39–56), and others are found in the book of Acts, they cumulatively constitute one of that relatively small number of thematic emphases which, considered together, give us our best clues to the situational context that originally constrained the composition of Luke–Acts as a whole. And at least in terms of the role played by women in this situation, the attitudes and values of the implied author of Luke–Acts have to be seen as dramatically different from those promulgated in the Pastoral Epistles, whatever correspondences or similarities might be established between them in other areas of context.

The rhetorical subordination of female chastity to the honour of male heroes

Although there is no reason to doubt that the author of Luke–Acts consciously wanted his depictions of Mary and Anna and the daughters of Philip to function in the ways discussed above, questions about how much weight this particular emphasis ought to be assigned – or about how it relates to other prominent emphases discernible in these writings – need to be asked if serious misinterpretations are to be avoided. As in all acts of interpretation, moreover, so in the present one the range and number of these questions are necessarily limited. Yet, by reflecting further on the last two features discussed above in connection with Luke's characterisation of Mary, it might be possible here to contextualise Luke's larger rhetoric of the ascetic woman in a way that enhances scholarly understanding of the interplay between text and context in Luke–Acts.

As hinted above, a wide range of strategies are employed in Luke 1.5–2.52 to communicate that Mary is greater than either Zechariah or Elizabeth. One factor, however, is perhaps more instrumental in achieving this elevation of Mary than all the others, namely the special prominence of this comparison in the scene of Mary's visit to Elizabeth (1.39–56). As outlined below and noted by René Laurentin and others, this particular episode not only occupies the central position in the scheme of parallels that constitute the structure of Luke 1.5–2.52 as a whole, but also – unlike each of the other episodes in this section – has no structural counterpart that might form a parallel to it.[24] These qualities unite to make the content of Luke 1.39–56 stand out in this section, with particularly strong emphasis falling on any motifs that are repeated either within the unit itself or by correspondence to elements in the immediate co-text.

The literary structure of Luke 1.5–2.52

  A. Anticipations: Announcements of Remarkable Births (1:5–38)
    1. The son of Zechariah and Elizabeth (1.5–26)
    2. The son of Mary (1.26–38)
  B. Story of Mary's Visit to Elizabeth (1.39–56)
    1. Elizabeth and her unborn son honour Mary (1:41–45)
    2. Mary praises the Lord (1.46–55)
  A.´ Fulfilments: Stories of Birth, Testimony, and Growth (1.57–2.52)
    1. John, the son of Zechariah and Elizabeth (1.57–80)
    2. Jesus, the son of Mary (2.1–52)

Yet the greatness of Mary *vis-à-vis* Zechariah and Elizabeth is not the only motif that is put in the foreground by these means. For the asymmetry noted above with reference to the interchange between Mary and Elizabeth does more than merely highlight discrepancies in status between Mary on the one hand and Elizabeth and Zechariah on the other. It also stresses, in ways which anticipate key developments in the larger narrative, that the fruit of Mary's womb will be greater than the son of her kinswoman (Luke 1.41–44).

As for the scope and character of these later developments, all that can be offered here is a selective summary. For instance, in the material on the Baptist's preaching in Luke 3.1–20, John addresses queries about his identity ('whether he might be the Messiah'; Luke 3.15) not merely by refusing to accept messianic status but by emphatically subordinating his own worth to that of Jesus (Luke 3.16). In a similar vein, and in contrast to the Markan and Matthean accounts of Jesus' baptism by John, the Lukan version (Luke 3.21–22) conspicuously puts in the background John's involvement in this event, with the baptism's human agent being deleted and John not being mentioned even once. Subsequent to this, moreover, when the status of the Baptist is addressed by Jesus himself (Luke 7.24–28), John's greatness is by no means denied – he is 'more than a prophet' (Luke 7.27) and preeminent 'among those born of women' (Luke 7.28) – yet, by virtue of his assumed role as the messianic age's precursor, his stature is less than that of even 'the least in the kingdom of God' (Luke 7.28).

But finally, and just as important as any of the elements surveyed above, three units in Luke's second volume contain interchanges that, especially when considered cumulatively, imply a context in which the baptism of John was being assigned a significance that the implied author of Acts considered inappropriate (Acts 1.4–5; 18.24–26; 19.2–5). Since the last two of these exchanges, moreover, instantiate a collocation of themes that are known to have co-occurred in the agonistic situation addressed by Paul in 1 Corinthians, namely baptismal practice and the influence of Apollos,[25] Luke's development of the John/baptism theme appears to reflect concerns that played no minor role in the challenges to his authority which Paul himself had confronted in the Corinthian correspondence.[26] In this light a question that deserves more sustained attention than scholarship has given it to date is whether Apollos's contribution to Paul's difficulties in Corinth included not only the impact of his rhetorically trained speaking but also an understanding of baptism that, at least from Paul's perspective, showed too much continuity with the custom of John.

Whatever interesting conjectures might be made in this latter connection, however, one point can be asserted here with confidence: in comparison with Luke's aforementioned emphasis on the positive potential of asceticism, his interest in subordinating John the Baptist to Jesus is demonstrably stronger. Indeed, while there is no need here to develop the point at length, one of Luke's primary aims in portraying Mary and her mode of conception as virginal in the first place was probably to accentuate Jesus' superiority to John. After all, as several of the allusions to the Septuagint (e.g. Gen. 18.9–15; Judg. 13.2–7; 1 Sam. 1.1–11) in Luke 1.5–25 confirm, John's birth was not unlike several other, earlier, well-known births in which the God of Israel had intervened; but conception by a virgin is an altogether different story.

Furthermore, and in view of the central role of Luke 1.39–56 in signalling the superiority of Mary to Zechariah and Elizabeth (and thus of Jesus to John), the parallelism of the surrounding units should almost certainly be read as conveying a very similar message. More specifically, as the structure of Luke 1.5–2.52 as a whole encourages the reader to compare the witness of the chaste and faithful Anna (Luke 2.36–38) with that given earlier by Zechariah (Luke 1.67–79), a contrast between these two figures emerges that is not unlike the difference encoded earlier between John and Jesus in Luke 3.15–17: Zechariah is important, not to mention capable of prophetic speech and insight, but he does not possess the merits of the chaste and ascetic Anna, especially after his failure to believe God's messenger (Luke 1.18–22, 59–62).

By means of this comparative elevation of the witness to Jesus, Luke further heightens the status of Jesus himself. And the point is given still greater emphasis through Luke's uneven distribution of the witnesses, with the many who bring honour to Jesus (Luke 2.8–52) outnumbering the sole attester to John (Luke 1.67–79). Consequently, what was concluded above regarding the rhetorical function of Mary's virginity may likewise be deduced concerning that of Anna's asceticism: while on one level it offers a model for imitation, on another level – one that is more direct, more emphatic, more rooted in agonistic immediacies – it serves to heighten the worth of Anna's witness to Jesus. And thus, ultimately, it enables Luke to accentuate in still another way the subordination of the Baptist to the central hero of the narrative.

Conclusion

Cumulatively, the force of Luke's representations of female virgins and other chaste women is much too strong to be dismissed as irrelevant to the social interests and tensions that shaped the production of Luke–Acts. The author of these two volumes included these images not simply because he inherited them from his 'tradition', but more importantly because he realised that they might bring forth desires in certain members of his audience to imitate the ascetic forms of commitment which these images commend. That this truly was one of Luke's aims, however, does not entail that this was his only, or even his most important, aim.

In the analysis above at least one of Luke's other goals has been identified, and it is one to which his interest in chaste women was carefully subordinated, with neither his greater nor his lesser commitments being seriously jeopardised. To be concise, Luke not only subordinates his interest in women's asceticism to his emphasis on Jesus' superiority to John, but he actually manages to employ it as a tool for underscoring the latter. In this perhaps more than in any other facet of Luke's narrative strategy, his ambivalent posture towards women is an index of the gender-political boundaries that he necessarily internalised from his cultural context: his rhetorically subtle and effective ways of appealing to women are, ultimately, subservient to highly conventional preoccupations with male contests over honour.

Despite this tension, however, and while Schopenhauer was probably not thinking of Luke's illustrious female ascetics when he penned the words cited at the beginning of this essay, his reference to 'women-veneration' probably has as one of its necessary cultural conditions the Lukan portrayal of Mary. Consequently, whatever moral and socio-cultural limitations may have been internalised by Luke himself, and in so far as his dangerous images of chaste women have helped to annoy the Schopenhauers of the world and inspire their political opponents, the reception history constituted by the effects that Luke's persuasive artistry has registered on his audiences has included more than its share of edifying moments.

Suggested further reading

MARGARET Y. MACDONALD, *Early Christian Women and Pagan Opinion: The Power of the Hysterical Woman* (Cambridge: Cambridge University Press, 1996).

CLARICE J. MARTIN, 'The Acts of the Apostles', *Searching the Scriptures: Volume Two: A Feminist Commentary* (ed. E. Schüssler Fiorenza; New York: Crossroad Publishing Company, 1994; London: SCM Press, 1995), pp. 763–99.

JAROSLAV PELIKAN, *Mary through the Centuries: Her Place in the History of Culture* (New Haven and London: Yale University Press, 1996).

TURID K. SEIM, *The Double Message: Patterns of Gender in Luke–Acts* (Studies of the New Testament and Its World; Edinburgh: T&T Clark, 1994).

KAREN J. TORJESEN, *When Women Were Priests: Women's Leadership in the Early Church and the Scandal of Their Subordination in the Rise of Christianity* (San Francisco: HarperCollins, 1993).

CHAPTER SEVEN

'THE STORY' AND 'OUR STORIES': NARRATIVE THEOLOGY, VERNACULAR RELIGION AND THE BIRTH OF JESUS

Elaine Graham

The birth of Jesus and cultural representation

My contribution to this collection of studies is less of a definitive essay than a suggestion for a research agenda. I want to locate my enquiries somewhere at the intersection of sociological studies of contemporary religion in Britain and practical theology, and to ask some questions about the ways in which religion – especially religious or sacred narratives – actually works for people. By that I mean the significance of such narratives in helping people construct worlds of meaning, perhaps in particular to make connections between their stories and the more overarching stories of faith-communities. I am, then, thinking about 'the birth of Jesus' not just as a textual or scriptural phenomenon, not just as a point of departure for Christian apologetics or doctrine, but as a form of *cultural representation*, or *cultural practice*.

I take my empirical material not from 'high culture', as in the study of the iconography of images of the birth of Jesus in visual art, for example.[1] Rather, I have chosen to address the birth of Jesus through the phenomenon of the nativity play. Perhaps the nearest historical parallel might be to think about the cultural significance of mystery plays, as simultaneously expositions of theological themes and expressions of popular piety. In so far as such cultural practices might be manifestations of broader social and political contexts, they might be said to reflect a kind of *vernacular* culture, if you like, that begins with a representation of the birth narrative but assumes an altogether more eclectic character.

The nativity play and the contemporary study of religion

The nativity play is, on one level, totally prosaic; but my hypothesis is that it serves to illuminate a number of important themes in the contemporary study of religion. We may regard these little events that take place in Christian churches, schools, community centres and elsewhere probably thousands of times every year, as harmless pieces of folk religion, a little sideshow for the children, fodder perhaps for the family photo or video album, but not of any lasting significance, let alone the subject of a hypothetical research agenda. I beg to differ. Nativity plays consume immense amounts of person hours. In some school contexts they are treated as significant educational activities; in a church-related context, they might be treated as integral to the Christian education and formation of young children, and a crucial aspect of the worshipping community's celebration of the Christmas festival. (A subsidiary research project, on the spirituality of young children who participate in nativity plays, also suggests itself at this point.)

In whatever setting it may take place, however it may be presented, there is at the heart of the nativity play an enactment of a religious narrative, albeit not necessarily in the context of public worship, nor involving (amongst cast or supporting crew) those who profess a religious conviction. It is more appropriately viewed as part of a general round of Christmas celebrations, but may, along with the carol service or possibly Christmas Eve/Christmas morning liturgies, be the nearest many (nominally Christian) people will come to participating in an act of organised religion all year. And that is perhaps another reason for studying the nativity play as a case study in the dynamics of 'believing and belonging':[2] as a microcosm of the wider meaning of the season of 'Christmas'. Of course, the phenomenon of 'Christmas' as celebrated in contemporary Britain is quite another matter from the birth of Jesus; but this observation only serves to illustrate my point. 'Christmas' is not purely a religious festival, but rather a hybrid: of Christian festival – focused on birth narratives – folk religion, consumerism, pre-Christian winter festivals, post-Dickensian sentimentality, and so on. So my imaginary research begins with a question that asks, What role does the *birth of Jesus* play in popular apprehension of the holiday season, and how is this articulated?

If we were to embark on an extended study of the nativity play, we would probably come to appreciate that its textual connection to the Gospel birth narratives is a matter of great variation. In the week before Christmas 1999, I attended two such plays. One took place in the context of public worship of the Church of Scotland, which followed a synthesis of the synoptic Gospel narratives, faithfully tracing the annunciation, the journey to Bethlehem, the stable, shepherds, angels, magi and the flight into Egypt. Each scene was interspersed with a short homily by a layperson and rounded off with a short children's sermon from the minister. The second play was at a rural nursery school in the West of England, where children and staff stage an annual spectacular based on the relatively secular theme of the four seasons. Despite this non-confessional emphasis, however, the final scene draws all the participants to the manger in Bethlehem.

The contrast between these two examples already generates important questions. Do nativity plays work from a set text? Can the nativity play stray beyond the boundaries of the biblical sources? In what ways is the narrative framed? What is the purpose of the annual process of telling and retelling? Let us confine ourselves, initially, to classifying the nativity play as a type of activity, religious or quasi-religious. It might be possible to compare the nativity play with other similar events and activities which ostensibly derive from Christian festivals but which have assumed a kind of heterodox, semi-independent status, such as harvest festivals, Remembrance Sunday, or May Queen celebrations.

Nativity plays as vernacular religion

My supposition awaiting validation would offer the suggestion that we consider nativity plays to be of a piece with these kinds of part-religious, part-popular events. Subsequent research might then locate nativity plays and other similar manifestations within some analytical framework or typology; something constructed by sociologists of religion, perhaps, to characterise the different patterns of religious affiliation and observance, expressions of orthodoxy/heterodoxy, institutional forms and varieties of ritual or devotional practice. A fourfold scheme might suffice: indicating a heuristic distinction between institutional, civil, popular and implicit religion, represented diagrammatically in Figure 1.[3]

Figure 1

'OFFICIAL RELIGION'

Institutional		*Civil*
Organised		
'BELIEF'		'PRACTICE'
Popular		*Implicit*
Common		*Surrogate*

'VERNACULAR RELIGION'

This typology has been constructed on the assumption that Britain today exhibits the empirical characteristics of an indigenous Christian (or nominally Christian) majority whose formal affiliation is declining rapidly (as incidentally is that of Anglo-Jewry). Alongside the indigenous Christian majority there is a significant presence of migrant communities from the Caribbean and South Asia who for the time being at least are retaining numerical and organisational strength. But of those who choose not to attend public worship or profess institutional membership, there is still – although the signs are that this is changing too – a great deal of non-affiliated support for religion. This phenomenon does seem to be a distinctively British manifestation in comparison to the rest of Europe and certainly to the United States – and if not universally British, then English, white, urban and working-class very markedly.

If we tried to locate the nativity play as a legitimate religious or quasi-religious event, I wonder where and according to what criteria we might categorise it within my basic typology. It might be classed as a form of *institutional or official religion*, if conducted in the context of public worship in a Christian context. *Civil religion* – the use of religious rituals and language in public life, especially ceremonial associated with the monarchy, the state and civic events – also has its allure, in so far as the nativity play might be seen as an expression of community life, a ritual affirmation of a shared culture. The nativity play might also be classed as *common religion*, a wide variety of heterodox and eclectic beliefs and practices pertaining to the supernatural, some derived from official religion, some predating Christianity – especially if we were to take my earlier comments about Christmas into account. In their diversity, their capacity to mould themselves around a local context or situation, nativity plays at their most eclectic and heterodox might well exemplify some of these traits.

Invisible, implicit or 'surrogate' religion are alternative terms for a more controversial set of practices, because there is great disagreement as to whether they constitute a category with any coherence, let alone credibility. They point to activities with no explicit religious or supernatural referent, but which by some aspect of their effect on participants and observers may engender a sense of the sacred or, as Emile Durkheim would have it, of 'collective effervescence'. Football, science fiction fandom, pilgrimages to sacred sites and political rallies have all been placed in this category – corporate activities in the main, but not necessarily mass events. For its critics, implicit religion represents the triumph of form and function over substance, and many would argue that as such these are not religious activities, since some kind of world-view or belief-system is necessary for any working definition of 'religion'. Certainly, the extent to which the nativity play retains a residual relationship to formal traditions and narratives of institutional Christianity suggests that this category is not particularly appropriate.

It is possible, however, that a programme of participant observation of nativity plays up and down the land would in fact uncover aspects of all these types. After all, my scheme is intended at this imaginary stage to be no more than a heuristic system anyway. But a research project into nativity plays might with good reason glance laterally at other contemporary phenomena which also embody elements of all these types, an empirical process which might result in significant adaptation of the theoretical construct itself. Studies of the response to the death of Lady Diana Spencer might acknowledge that it, too, contained elements of official (formal Christian observance and liturgy), civil (the state funeral), common (the elements of popular music at the heart of the funeral service itself) and surrogate (diffuse expressions of grief in the vernacular of lighted candles and floral tributes)[4] forms of religion.

Here, perhaps, it may be most illuminating to use a heuristic scheme such as that in Figure 1 to advance an understanding of religious belief and practice in contemporary Britain as best understood as part of human cultural activity. Religion may thereby be seen as one amongst many 'cultural resources'[5] by which people build a world or worlds: worlds of meaning, celebration, mourning, obligation, and so on. I take my idea of human beings as builders of worlds from the work of William Paden, who argues that 'religious worlds' are the material and symbolic systems people build through ritual, through myth, through patterns of purity and pollution, through representations of their God or gods.[6] The function of religion as cultural resource is thus one of providing means by which people can engage in the creation of what Thomas Luckmann called a 'moral universe of meaning'. Whilst organised religion may constitute one particular external source of authority by which some kinds of moral universes are handed on, there are perhaps signs of greater latitude in the choice of moral universes that are built in a post-Christian society, as the bonds that connect people to those institutions loosen.[7]

Again, to consider the proposition that nativity plays are one small cultural resource – one part of the story-telling and myth-making that is necessary for individual and collective life – might entail placing this in wider sociological context. These themes of fragmentation, of dissipation of formal narratives and teachings of official religion, being replaced by more eclectic and personalised tools and resources, is familiar territory; but in order to introduce a little originality into the analysis, I might avoid discussion of 'postmodernity' and talk instead about mobility and fluidity as the core characteristic of twenty-first-century western societies. Geographical, social, occupational, familial and virtual[8] mobility means that people are much more fluid in their allegiances and life-styles – a condition of *bricolage*, perhaps. A religious or existential mobility would be consistent with such an analysis, so that in thinking about the narratives, resources, icons, values and institutions that shape the worlds people build, it would be clear that inherited religious narratives would have to take their turn alongside other 'sacred' and exemplary stories in our culture, represented by science, consumerism and the media.

Nativity plays as narrative theology

Intentionally, I am moving gradually into another important area of this imagined research around the birth of Jesus and the significance of narrative, religious or otherwise. Human experience is frequently narrative experience. The key medium through which such worlds are built, how people inhabit them, how order is brought to a chaotic world, may be through the telling of stories. Narrative – whether myth, fairy tale or 'talking cure' – is part of the fundamental fabric of human identity.[9] A dialogue with those working in the field of narrative theology would be fruitful as we considered the relationship between people's individual stories, the collective story – especially those taking place in vernacular forms such as nativity plays – and 'The Story', or the Christian story. For the narrative theologian, the Christian gospel is not abstract propositional doctrine distilled from its narrative roots. The narrative is the truth, and vice versa. Hans Frei spoke of the 'indispensible narrative web' making up the texture of story, context, tellers and hearers of a story. The narrative builds a world, therefore, into which the hearer must step in order to apprehend the moral logic that underlies the story.

But for many narrative theologians, 'The Story' is Scripture, God's narratives; and these must be treated as paradigmatic, definitive for the community of faith. So 'The Story' absorbs and corrects 'our stories'; as Gerard Loughlin has it, 'in the sense of making oneself over to its narrative in order to be made anew'.[10] 'The Story' encounters our stories and reads the human situation accordingly. But it is clear that the tradition takes precedence; as George Stroup argues, 'revelation occurs when the Christian narrative collides with personal identity and the latter is recon-structed by means of the former'.[11] 'To enter the world of the Scripture', says Gerard Loughlin, 'to become a part of its story, is to enter the community that reads the Scripture as that which delineates the world of the community; it is to become a part of the community's own story.'[12]

However, I want to interpose, 'but who is telling whose story, who is defending the boundaries of the community, whose voices are excluded and silenced?' I doubt that 'The Story' has the predominance or definitive status often assumed by many (not all) narrative theologians. The self-sufficiency and exclusivity of the Christian narrative for the building of worlds is, I think, misguided, for a number of reasons. First, the sociological evidence defies the self-sufficiency of religious narrative, mistakenly assumed to be independent of its context, or of Christian faith hermetically sealed from the sensibilities of folk religion. Second, theologically speaking, an incarnational faith would suggest that God's story is embodied in and through human communities who are enjoined to watch and wait for the coming of the kingdom in unexpected, even heterodox, places. Third – an obvious issue – there is the matter of the primacy and unity of 'The Story'. After Jean-François Lyotard, we may wonder whether the idea of the metanarrative, religious or otherwise, has any purchase. For deconstructionists, no narrative is a transparent telling-forth. Meaning is elusive, deferred and problematic; all stories fragment into intertextuality and artifice.

Finally, the implied hegemony of 'The Story' also gives concern to some. Are there absences or silences in 'The Story'? Does 'The Story' do violence to my, our stories? This is the position taken by the practitioners of many theologies of liberation, for example, who would argue that the canonical story is too exclusive to absorb and 'reconstruct' their hidden stories. Some narrative theologians take this in their stride, finding invisible witnesses between the lines and in the margins of the dominant story, and restoring them to the main text; or telling the story differently, taking issue with the boundaries of the text and changing the way it is told. Some of these writers, emphasising the fluidity of narrative, have indeed retold elements of the nativity story, such as Heather Walton in her retelling of the annunciation.[13] Whilst the popular nativity play is not engaged in deconstructing 'The Story' in quite such a way, there may nevertheless be a kind of implicit negotiation underway with the original story that transforms it from the sacred sanctioned text into something that lodges more in the realm of popular affection and popular religiosity, a transposition from 'The Story' to 'our story/ies'.

Conclusion

Potentially, attention to nativity plays as enactments of the birth of Jesus illuminates the performative dimensions of religion, and of religious narrative in particular. In a variety of settings, with a cast of thousands, year in year out, stories of the birth of Jesus are enacted by ordinary people. I have tried to indicate why we might consider the humble nativity play to be first, a kind of popular or vernacular religion, and second whether we might class it as an elementary form of narrative theology. I have suggested that nativity plays might, as a kind of thought-experiment-cum-research proposal, chart a course through some contemporary debates about the dynamics of religious believing and belonging, as well as inviting us to think about the capacity of human beings to be builders of worlds – and tellers of stories.

Suggested further reading

GRACE DAVIE, *Religion in Britain since 1945: Believing Without Belonging* (Oxford: Blackwell, 1994).

GERARD LOUGHLIN, *Telling God's Story: Bible, Church and Narrative Theology* (Cambridge: Cambridge University Press, 1996).

IV

JESUS:
FULLY SYMBOLIC AND MORE

CHAPTER EIGHT

AN ICONOLOGICAL ARGUMENT

F. Gerald Downing

Nativity and incarnation

We have lots of images of the nativity of Jesus – stable, manger, beasts, shepherds, kings (or are they wizards?). Here I discuss images and imagination. 'Icon' is a Greek word for image, especially for the sacred images in worship. What follows is a reflection on images and imagination: an iconological argument.

It may well seem that originally virgin birth and incarnation (as we have come to term them) were alternatives. In Matthew and in Luke as they stand, and despite the genealogies, Jesus has no human progenitor; Mary receives a specially created seed, and provides the fertile field in which it grows, and that is the starting point for this Son of God. Rather differently, John (John 7.42) and Hebrews (Heb. 7.14) and Paul (Rom. 1.3; 9.5) suggest a starting point for the Son of God prior to his taking on a human life, but a human life which *was* of the seed of Abraham and of David.

Nonetheless, historically the two motifs became combined, and then a genetic break – a break in the line of original sin – becomes a constituent element of the doctrine. Clearly many Christians now take it that the narrated virginal birth (or conception) of Jesus is a necessary part of any full story of incarnation. And this – incarnation – is what matters. Without 'incarnation' I doubt whether a special nativity of Jesus would be much discussed, by us or others. It is believed in Islam on the authority of the Koran, but is not, I think, a subject of much theological reflection among Moslems. Anyway, I am going to discuss incarnation, as the wider context within which our theme, the birth of Jesus, is traditionally set.

I take it that many Christians and sympathetic others find '*in-carnation*' difficult to make sense of, even with or especially with the help of popular films in which people swap bodies or invade other bodies. I think it is worth noting that Christian ideas of Jesus as an incarnate pre-existent divine being grew up in a culture which both entertained such suggestions – and knew how daft they could sound in some ears. Christians persisted in developing ideas of incarnation even though they were aware of some of the puzzles which still puzzle us.

A popular entertainer, Lucian of Samosata (mid-second century CE) offers us an imaginary conversation in Hades between Diogenes the Cynic and the god-man Herakles, taken to be son by Zeus of Alcmena, wife of Amphitryon. Lucian is probably recasting a satire by the Cynic writer, Menippus (from Gadara, near Galilee, mid-second century BC).

> D: Herakles, isn't it? By Herakles, it can't be anyone else. There's the bow, the club, the lionskin . . . the expanse. It's Herakles to a T. So, a son of Zeus – and dead! Tell me, mighty victor, are you really dead? Back on earth I used to offer sacrifices to you as a god.

> H: Quite right, too, those sacrifices. The divine Herakles you offered them to is in heaven, among the gods, 'with lovely-limbed Hebe' for wife. I'm just his phantom.

> D: How come? A phantom of deity? Can someone really be half-divine and half-deceased?

> H: That Herakles isn't dead, it's only me that's dead, his phantom.

> D: I see now. He's given you to Pluto as his stand-in, so you're dead instead of him.

H: Sort of.

D: Aeachus is usually very particular. How was it he didn't notice that you weren't him, and went and admitted a substitute Herakles when you turned up?

H: Because I look exactly like him.

D: True enough, you do look exactly like him, you could very well be him. But maybe it's just the other way round. It's you who's Herakles, and it's the phantom who's shacked up with Hebe in heaven?

H: Bloody nerve! you with your big mouth. If you don't watch out, taking the piss, I'll show you what sort of god I'm phantom to.

D: His bow is out, and strung. But why should I worry? I'm dead already, once and for good. Still, in the name of your Herakles, when he was alive on earth, were you there, along with him, as his phantom? Or were the two of you one then, and split up when you both died, so he went up to the gods and you came down here where you belong, in Hades?

H: I've no need to reply if you won't take things seriously. Still, you just listen. All that Amphitryon contributed to Herakles died – and all of that's me. What Zeus contributed is up there with the gods.

D: Now it's coming clear. What you're saying it that Alkmena gave birth to two Herakleses at the same time, one by Amphitryon and one by Zeus, but no one realised they were twins from the same mother?

H: No, stupid, we were both the same person.

D: No, that's not easy to make sense of, two Herakleses synthesised. Not unless you were a human and a god spliced from birth like a Centaur, half human, half horse.

H: Don't we all seem to be like that, a combination of two elements, soul and body? So what prevents the soul bit –

the bit from Zeus – being in heaven, and me being the
mortal bit, here among the dead?

D: But, most respected son of Amphitryon, that would be fine
if you were here bodily. But you're a disembodied phantom.
This way you risk tripling Herakles.

H: What d'you mean, tripling?

D: Well, it's like this. If there's one in heaven, and one here –
that's you, the phantom – and there's a body on Oeta,
gone to dust, we've got three Herakleses. And you need to
start looking to find a third father, too, to be responsible
for the body.[1]

Lucian's contemporary, Justin Martyr, makes it clear that
Christians acknowledged the analogies. 'When we say that the
Word, the firstborn of God, was born without sexual union
. . . we propound nothing different from what you believe of
those you take to be sons of Zeus.'[2] In fact Christians often
themselves repeated such Cynic mockery of 'pagan' theology. Yet
despite the pagan analogies and the intellectual puzzles, Christians
went on elaborating and refining their faith in Jesus as God
incarnate.

The story as a narrated ideal

Many of us still don't find it easy to cope with such suggestions.
And yet some, and I myself for sure, find that we have been
drawn into imagining a three-person creative sustaining God
whose encompassing love extends to one of the three persons
sharing our life, bodily, and specifically as that elusive Jesus of
Nazareth. And having been taken by this ideal icon of deity,
any other God-talk seems insipid, jejune by comparison – to
some of us.

Maybe nonetheless the best we can then do with such stuff is
to talk of the divine being born in us (after all, the carols of the
nativity do that, and Grace Jantzen argues it powerfully)[3] and
then perhaps we could maintain some of the traditional images, if

they do retain some grip on our imaginations, as a picture way of expressing an ideal of love, openness to others, generosity, creativity ... and even judgement. And, with many others, I have long been convinced myself that there is no way of *showing* that God talk – this or any alternative – is other than the expression of a personified, dramatised ideal.

The traditions that hold me focus on Jesus, however variously interpreted, and on this Jesus as the expression in person of the creative and sustaining and enabling love of God. God is integral to the story of Jesus in the tradition that holds me, and Jesus alive is integral to the story of God that constitutes the ideal that continues to grip me – in some measure. I still cannot show that it is more than a story, an ideal narrated: but something like that is the story, articulates the ideal.

The ideal that Jesus-within-the-ongoing-diverse-tradition presents me with includes integrally the divine persons-in-relation, actively relating to one another, and so drawing us, drawing me into the divine life, the divine love: love enabling and welcoming love. But that could still leave me with a three-personed God imagined as imaginary. My further argument is that that is not enough, nor need that be all.

Ideals as icons or icons as idols

How is my ideal better than an idol? You may have heard it said that mental images are more dangerous than metal ones. Of course I can say, I did not create this icon out of nothing, it is in that sense not simply mine. And I could say, I listen to others, I read their writings, engage in their dramas, see their pictures: so my icon, my vision, is alive, is not a dead idol, in that sense at least. Nor is my ideal simply a projection of myself, a deified self-image: it really does both judge and draw me from beyond my own resources.[4]

Well, that is important – especially if it is even only in small measure true. But my vision remains mine, it is I who fashion and maybe refashion it. Am I condemned, even in imagination, to be the typical self-made Englishman who worships his creator? Serving an ideal of my own creating that I acknowledge as my creation despite others' contributions leaves me still a sort of idolater. The second Isaiah's idol-maker did not work on his own, either, but was still an idolater in the prophet's eyes (Isa. 40.6–7, 18–20).

The imagined real and the imagined unreal

I read a novel in which characters confront hopes and fears. They imagine dangers, they imagine rescue. Sometimes the danger is itself imaginary, imaginary within the text; so, too, the succour. Within the narrative imaginary lions are terrifying, even disabling; imaginary saviours inspire real hope. But only real lions eat people, in the narrative; only a real squadron of cavalry saves the wagon-train. Imagined villains (or friends' imagined villainy) can destroy peace of mind, in the story; imagined friends (or real enemies' imagined kindness) may afford consolation. Only friends who are real in the story – are imagined in the story as real – can have a real relationship with other characters in the story. Only real friends, real in the telling, can touch and caress and provide food; only they can be the spontaneous 'other' who gives and receives caring and creative (or, indeed, destructive) attention. It makes a great difference within the story whether others within the story are imagined as imaginary or imagined as real.[5]

The grace of the other imagined-as-real

It makes a great difference to the ideal I treat as divine and call our three-personed God if I imagine God as real rather than imagine God as imaginary. It makes a great difference to the imagining. Only as I imagine God as real can I imagine God as parent, 'thou' to my 'I'; only as I imagine God as sibling, born my brother, can that imagined-as-real divine Word and Wisdom initiate and respond, share in the relationship. Only so can the Spirit blow (or can it be imagined really to blow) where she will, and not just where I choose to send him. Only so can the imagined three-person God draw us, draw me, into the creative, loving reciprocity of the divine life together. Only so can the ideal live up to the ideal . . . and perhaps not be my idol.

I recall Dennis Potter's *Hide and Seek*, a novel in which characters gain a life of their own, or at least, seem to.[6] Perhaps that might seem enough to allow the God I imagine as an ideal the otherness, the alterity that allows a graciousness, a giftedness, a surprising light and lightness, an effective vividness. And perhaps not an idol simply of my making. Well, in the writing this essay ran its own course in that sort of way, it was not sketched in detail before I started. But, of course, I did know some of the things I wanted to say, even if the ways of writing them emerged – for good or ill – without detailed forward planning. And that is how words appear, anyway; some words create the possibility or impossibility, the likelihood or unlikelihood of other words to follow, whether uttered by me or by you. Using language involves being prepared for a manageable range of compossible sequences, and the one that emerges does seem at times to speak itself (or, as some would insist, does seem to speak me). But finding what I think only when I hear myself say it or see myself write it is still not the same as reading someone else's novel, or having a co-author for my own. Imagining the God of my ideal as real is different – importantly different – from imagining the God of my ideal as imaginary.

This 'iconological' argument is meant to suggest slight echoes of Anselm of Bec's 'ontological' one, which reminds us that the God of Judeao-Christian religion is 'by definition' real.[7] It also has something in common with other suggestions that deny that doctrinal statements are making 'factual' claims, but rather constitute the 'grammar' of worship, or are 'regulative' of it.[8] I think my suggestion goes deeper into a phenomenology of grace, of the kind of relational ethic that Christian tradition variously invites and claims to afford.

Imagining the divine Word identifying
with Jesus of Nazareth.

Can one then write a coherently imaginable story of one person
of the three-person God living the life of a somewhat out of the
ordinary and for us rather elusive male Galilaean peasant carpenter?
I tried to sketch a positive response some thirty years ago, in a
book entitled *A Man for Us and a God for Us* (though it only
touched in passing on the matter of the social construction of
gender, and other potentially distancing matters).[9] My suggestion
deployed aspects of the open set of analogies which I have been
deploying here. There are levels of identifying with a character on
stage, in a novel, 'in real life'. One accepts that such identification
may be neurotic, psychotic. But it may be deliberate, positive,
measured – and still intense. For a while you are that person,
crying, puzzling, deceiving, hurting, laughing, sweating, aroused,
exhilarated, depressed.

The only ideal that works for me as a Christian disciple in the
way outlined, works within the Christian tradition and demands
just such a narrative, in which a person of the three-personed
God identified exhaustively with the entire life of a not quite
ordinary but quite credible Galilaean peasant some two thousand
years ago, from – well, probably – from an ordinary conception
to a sadistic death. This was God, the divine Word, accepting the
dreaming innocence of the womb, becoming sensitised to his
mother's heart-beat, digestion, moods, movements; to the anguish
of birth, the grief of separation, the coming to self-awareness; to
ignorance, hunger, the pleasures of fresh bread and local wine; to
love, friendship, disappointment. That sort of formation, however
one imagines it: one shaped by Mary who carried him, gave birth
to him, reared him, shaped by Joseph, by sisters and brothers, by
the village community and its traditions. The Word took that
risk – and the risk of all the good and the bad and the sheer
diversity that ensues. In most versions of the story that articulate
a Christian ideal the Word of God was (still is) Jesus, the
identification continues; and in that sense, but only in that sense,

in the story, Jesus, quite unawares, was God. In the story, told like this, he shared our life so we might share the divine life.

As I have insisted, I cannot show, so I have found no one else who can show that this or any variant is other than imaginary, even though I imagine it among others who entertain the same story, or recognisable variants of it. I have to say, for me the virginal conception weakens this story; an ordinary genetic inheritance for Jesus (as in Paul and others, seed of Abraham and of David) affords a stronger narrative, where Mary is still more fully Theotokos (while Joseph, of course, in this telling, would share the title).[10] But I urge, the story – whichever version you entertain – is only worth imagining if you imagine it to be true.

Suggested further reading

F. L. CROSS (ed.), *The Oxford Dictionary of the Christian Church*; the third edition for preference, re-edited by E. A. Livingstone; (Oxford: Oxford University Press, 1998), and articles there: 'Icon', p. 815; 'Incarnation', pp. 825–6; 'Trinity', pp. 1641–2; 'Anselm', pp. 73–4; 'Ontological', p. 1184; 'Christology', pp. 336–8.

C. E. GUNTON (ed.), *The Cambridge Companion to Christian Doctrine* (Cambridge: Cambridge University Press, 1997), chapter 7, R. D. Colle, 'The Triune God', pp. 121–40 and chapter 13, K. Tanner, 'Jesus Christ', pp. 245–72.

J. PELIKAN, *Imago Dei* (Princeton: Princeton University Press, 1990), on icons.

CHAPTER NINE

NATIVITY AND NATALITY

Grace M. Jantzen

The premise: birth or death?

Christendom, and with it western civilisation, premises itself upon a birth. It was through a birth, according to Christian teaching, that the divine entered the world. Whatever one's theology, whether one believes that Jesus was God incarnate, the Second Person of the Trinity, or whether one believes only that in Jesus we see more clearly than in most human beings what the divine is like, it all started with a birth. If we think that Jesus is in *any* sense revelatory, that revelation begins with his nativity: Jesus' nativity, whatever else it indicates, shows that in the pain and trauma and blood of childbirth, the divine is present.

And yet Christendom has made surprisingly little of it. We celebrate Christmas, of course; and we have recently celebrated the millennium, the two-thousandth anniversary, give or take a bit, of the birth of Jesus. But the theological focus of Christendom has been much more towards the death of Jesus than towards his birth. According to some variants of Christian theology, in fact, Jesus' birth is hardly significant in itself; it matters only as a means to an end, and that end is his death (and resurrection) for human redemption. Even for Christians who take a more liberal theological stance, the death of Jesus is often seen as paradigmatic of the divine: on the cross is revealed for all to see the love and compassion, justice and vulnerability of God.

Now, I don't want to enter into a discussion about which if
any of the variants of Christian doctrine are correct, nor do I
want to deny the significance of Jesus' death. What I want to do
instead is to ask, haven't we forgotten something? What about
birth? What if we were to take Jesus' nativity as seriously as his
death? Throughout the western tradition, mortality – the fact
that we all die – has been taken as central to our self-understanding,
while natality – the fact that we are all born – has been largely
ignored. 'All men are mortal' is the first premise of the first
syllogism of Introductory Logic: why not sometimes 'All people
are natals'? Those who have heard me lecture or read some of my
recent writings know that I am working on a large project tracing
the genealogy of mortality as a category of the western symbolic,
and its subversion by traces of natality. What I want to do in this
essay is to show how, right at the beginning of Christian tradition,
the nativity of Jesus already destabilises the notion of mortality as
a foundational category, and indicates something of the potential
of natality.

Death and hopelessness

What would the world be like if births decreased dramatically or
ceased altogether? In recent years several novelists have made that
question the premise of a book, notably Margaret Atwood in *The
Handmaids Tale*[1] and P. D. James in *The Children of Men*.[2] For
all the differences between these two books, both paint a chilling
picture. The population gets steadily older, and the resources to
care for the elderly are simply not available: drastic measures are
enacted. In Atwood's novel, the reason for the decrease in births
is that most women, especially in the upper classes, have become
infertile. The few women who might bear children are made
slaves of the rich and powerful, to breed for them, in a state system
that couples the most extreme form of Orwellian totalitarianism
with a Christian fundamentalism built up from a 'right-to-life'
approach: the land is called 'Gilead' and the breeding women are
'Handmaids' to the rich; from time to time all join in a

'Prayvaganza' which probably includes ritual executions of those who deviate. In P. D. James' scenario, it is the men who are infertile. Without children and young people, the world sinks increasingly into depression punctuated with violence. Above all, there is no hope: no hope for the world, no hope for a future, no newness entering the world. There is novelty, yes: ever more clever technology and gadgetry chiefly used for oppressive purposes. But real newness, real creativity of thought and action, has ceased. Death is all there is left.

Imagine a world in which no babies have been born for thirty years. People in their thirties and forties beg older folk to tell them what it used to be like: children shouting in a swimming bath or on the playing fields; children around the Christmas tree; children learning to read and write and wide-eyed with wonder at the world they are discovering. Imagine the disbelief, if there were no more children, that governments had once spent vast amounts on armaments and warfare but could not find the money for children's education – and now there are no children left. Imagine the horror at reports that children were sometimes abused, or kept in poverty. Imagine the desperation as scientists try to develop human cloning, and the corruption and political horrors to which society would be prone as the rich and powerful tried against all possibility to control the future. Above all, imagine the hopelessness.

Nativity and natality

When we have allowed ourselves to sink into a scenario like that, we can see more clearly the significance of natality as a category in our lives and our symbolic structures. A little later I shall suggest with a little more specificity some of the aspects of that significance. First, though, I want to ponder a little the importance of *nativity*, that is the actual fact of birth, for *natality* as a conceptual category. Birth, after all, is not the only way in which, in principle, new life can come into the world. Cloning is a steadily approaching possibility, for example: already governments are exercised about what the legal boundaries should be to scientific potential in this regard. As things now stand, cloning (as in the case of Dolly the sheep) still requires gestation: it is the embryo that is cloned and inserted into the womb, and the new individual is born and begins its life as an infant, just like anyone else. At present it is hard to see how one could produce an immediately adult individual through cloning.

But what about through information technology? It would be a rash philosopher who would dismiss out of hand the possibilities that one day maybe quite soon it will be possible to construct machines that will think, feel, be able to make choices and moral decisions, enter into relationships, and possibly even reproduce themselves. On what grounds could we say that they are not human? Biologically, of course, they are not. But unless we are biological reductionists – a position I consider incompatible with any sort of religious stance – I can see no reason to deny that just because there are microchips where we have blood vessels and nerves, they are not human beings with human rights and responsibilities. I have many worries about who would be constructing these beings, and for what purposes; and about who would be making decisions about them; but I can see no reason to rule in advance that such beings are not persons just because they have not come into the world through gestation and birth.

But why am I talking about twenty-first-century computer technology and genetic engineering in relation to the nativity of Jesus? The point is this: Jesus entered the world, not as an adult, but through birth and infancy. Moreover the birth narratives are emphasised by two of the Gospel writers. Now, if you hold to a high Christology, then you would have to say this represents the divine will: God *chose* that Jesus should enter the world as a baby even though he could have come fully grown. If on the other hand your understanding of Jesus is not in those high terms, this still leaves the issue of the emphasis on the nativity in the Gospel narratives' mythology. In some ways it would have been doctrinally tidier, whatever view of Jesus one holds, if these stories of Jesus' birth had been omitted, perhaps replaced by a story of his arrival on earth fully grown. Jesus was, after all, portrayed as a second Adam, a new man who would undo the damage caused by the first Adam. But the first Adam was never a baby. According to the Genesis story God formed him, and later Eve his wife, as fully adult. So to keep the parallel, shouldn't Jesus have arrived as an adult too?

But Jesus was born. There was a nativity. Shuffle as we may around the stories of angels and magi and shepherds and stars, to say nothing of a virgin mother, it would be pretty hard to deny that Jesus came into the world through birth and infancy, like any other human being. So if Jesus shows us something of what it means to be human, and perhaps even shows us something of what it means to be divine, part of what he shows is a validation of birth, of natality. Even if humankind learns to bring persons into the world in other ways, perhaps bypassing birth, the fact of Jesus' birth and its emphasis in the Gospels is surely intended as significant, even revelatory, for our thinking about ourselves and about the divine.

Natal features

So what does Jesus' nativity signify about natality? What does it mean to be natal? I leave open the extent to which some or all of these features could also be true of persons who entered the world through engineering, and to what extent therefore they could be considered 'honorary natals'. I shall suggest four features of natality, each of which I believe to be theologically significant, and each of which destabilises the preoccupation with death and mortality which has characterised the western tradition.[3]

Embodiment

First, natality entails embodiment. To be born is to be embodied, enfleshed. In Christendom the embodiment of Jesus is referred to as 'incarnation'; and as usual there are plenty of conflicting doctrines and theories about it. Rather than get into them, however, I again want to step back and consider the obvious: what is significant, even revelatory, about being embodied?

I can best arrive at this by contrast with mortality. Throughout Christian history, and with a lot of help from Plato, death has been thought of as in some sense the separation of the soul from the body, even if soul and body are thought to come together again in a resurrection for final judgement. The soul is what is important. This has had several consequences. First, it changes the focus to the eternal destiny of the soul, in some *other* world, away from the flourishing of the whole person in *this* world. Second, and connected with this, it means that the religious emphasis is on salvation of the soul for this other world, rather than on the welfare of human beings in this one. Third, in the west, the soul has been closely linked with the mind, with rationality, which has been valorised as humankind's most godlike attribute. It has also gone along with a construction of gender in which maleness is associated with rationality and the soul, while femaleness has been linked with bodiliness and reproduction. Since detachment of the soul from the body, or at least from bodily desires, has been linked with rationality and salvation, it is not hard to see how these constructions tend towards a denial of the religious significance of the body, the earth, and human justice and flourishing, while emphasising a rationality and spirituality somehow separate from the body and the physical. Moreover, it would not be saying too much to say that in much of the focus on mortality in the western tradition, and on the mortification (literally 'putting to death') of the flesh as spiritual discipline, there has been a deep undercurrent of misogyny.

An emphasis on natality subverts all that. Without denying the possibility of life after death, and certainly without denying that we will die, a focus on natality shows the significance of embodiment and our bodily life here and now. It shows that the flourishing of human beings requires that bodily needs must be met, and therefore that it is wholly misguided to bypass issues of justice and liberation and appropriate distribution of the world's resources in favour of a spirituality focused on salvation of a soul for some other world. Surely it is significant for our conception of the divine that in all the Gospel accounts in which Jesus met someone in physical distress he never told them that their bodily suffering was good for their soul, or even that it was unimportant in the light of eternity. On the contrary, he fed them or helped them or healed them, and often let them go their way without so much as a comment recorded about their souls or salvation for a future life.

Moreover, the idea that rationality is akin to godliness, let alone the idea that rationality can be detached from bodiliness, does not come from Jesus. If, as I am suggesting, the nativity of Jesus affirms the significance of natality, then our embodiment is to be celebrated not denigrated, and the embodied flourishing of all our fellow natals must have a high priority in our ethical and political stance. Neither does a focus on natality allow for the gender distortion whereby men are kept from being in touch with their bodies and emotions, while women are treated as sex objects and kept from exercising their rational capacities. Although the churches have often behaved shamefully toward women, there is no warrant for such behaviour in the incarnation that follows upon Jesus' natality.

Gender

This discussion anticipates the second feature of natality that I wish to emphasise: all natals are gendered. Well yes, of course: did we ever think otherwise? In a way, this is something we know very well; yet I suggest that, as with many obvious things, it is easy to miss its significance. Certainly Christendom has been missing its significance for many centuries, again by its focus on spiritual salvation and life after death in which, it is held, gender does not matter. The biblical warrant for that view seems to me to be remarkably thin, resting largely on Jesus' saying that in heaven there is no such thing as marriage, because people are 'like the angels'. Now unless one has already *assumed* that angels are genderless and have no sexual relations – and where is the warrant for that assumption? – then surely this passage could as easily be read as suggesting that in heaven sexual relations are free, not restricted by marriage as they are on earth.

Be that as it may, for embodied natals gender is inescapable and of great importance. Just think what happens whenever we hear that someone has had a baby. One of the things we want to know – even if the people are strangers, friends of friends, and it's nothing to do with us – is, 'Is it a girl or a boy?' Why do we want to know? Why is that question one of the first we ask? Or again, have you never found yourself walking down a street or sitting in a train and taking a hard second look at someone – a total stranger – because you had not ascertained their gender at first glance. I have; and have also asked myself why; what is it to do with me? Why should it matter? And yet we as if by instinct find gender and gender identification important. Indeed it is one of the more convoluted ironies of the west that even when we do not need to do so for warmth, we wear clothes for 'decency', at least enough to cover our genitals, even though gender signals are among the most insistent that we give and receive, and mistakes can cause us deep confusion.

Christendom has not had much to say about the significance of gender, though it has had plenty to say about the repression or regulation of sexual activity as well as about the subordination of women. But if gender, as an aspect of natality, is a cause to celebrate, then it is of the first importance that gender issues are given theological attention in a way that enhances the gender identification of women as well as men. No human can flourish who is oppressed because of their gender. Moreover I would argue that if Jesus shows the divine, then Jesus' embodiment, gendered as male, shows that gender identity is given divine validation. Need it be said that from this it does *not* follow that maleness is given a higher validation than femaleness? Surely what is important is not that Jesus was male rather than female, any more than that he was Jewish rather then Gentile. What matters is that he was fully human, a natal, and therefore particular rather than general in gender and in race.

The web of relation

This leads me to a third characteristic of natality, linked to its particularity. To be natal means to be part of a web of relationships, both diachronous and synchronous: it means, negatively, that atomistic individualism is not possible for natals. For all our particularity, we are particular and special primarily in relation to one another, not by ourselves alone. We could not survive, as infants, if we were not held and cared for in human nexus. Ancient Romans if they did not want to receive a new-born into the family or community abandoned it on a field of hillside: such exposed infants soon died.

In modernity in the west there has been a strong emphasis on independence and self-sufficiency, especially emotional self-sufficiency, as a mark of adult masculinity. Women who do not want stereotypical 'feminine weakness' sometimes take it on too. It goes along with an ethos of mastery and control: control of one's own body and emotions, and often also control of other people, thereby placing them in a role whereby they are perceived as dependent and as demeaned by that dependency. One need only think how Black slave men were regularly called 'boys' by their masters, or of how some men think of women as 'girls' who could not manage on their own. Again, the churches have often colluded with such attitudes, and reinforced them by, for example, referring to priests as 'father'.

But if Jesus' birth is in any sense revelatory of the divine, then one of the things it indicates is that there is such a thing as appropriate dependency and vulnerability, that we are part of a web of life and relationship. It seems that Jesus did not always get on well with members of his immediate family. Moreover he certainly took responsibility for himself and his actions already from the age of twelve, according to the story of his visit to the Jerusalem temple; and he placed a high value upon solitude. But all that is quite different from the sort of person who pretends to be emotionally invulnerable, and tries to control others as a disguise for their own inadequacy. Jesus' whole life showed his

interdependence with other people, from the fragility of his birth
to his last supper with his friends, even while also showing how
appropriate interdependence builds up rather than belittles
everyone concerned. Even in Gethsemane Jesus is portrayed as
repeatedly asking for emotional support from his friends. Jesus'
nativity affirms the significance of the web of interrelationship as
a characteristic of natality, and his life is a model of how such
connection can be lived without distortion.

Hope and possibility

Finally, to my mind the most significant feature of natality is that
it allows for hope. With each new infant, new possibilities are
born, new freedom and creativity, the potential that this child
will help make the world better. I would suggest that those characteristics – freedom, creativity, the potential for a fresh start –
are central to every human life and are ours in virtue of the fact
that we are natals. Hannah Arendt, pondering natality, saw it as
the aspect of the human condition which allows for the possibility
of making new beginnings, fresh starts whether large or small.
One of her favourite citations was from Augustine's *City of God*,
which she translated as, 'That a beginning might be made, man
was created, before whom nobody was.'[4] She argued, as I do here,
that 'because he *is* a beginning, man can begin; to be human and
to be free are one and the same. God created man in order to
introduce into the world the faculty of beginning: freedom'.[5] This
potential for making fresh starts, for acting creatively, is grounded
not in our mortality but in our embodied, gendered selfhood,
and is situated in the social and cultural web of relationships that
delineate our natality.

Once again, Jesus' nativity reinforces and validates this hope-
fulness of renewed possibility, of creative newness in embodied
natality. Whatever one's theology, the birth of Jesus is a symbol
of hope; it points towards new and better ways of living, more
just social and economic arrangements, more sensitivity and
integrity in interrelationships based on mutuality and respect rather

than control. 'For unto us a child is born . . .' It is birth, at least as much as death, that defines what it means to be human, natality that signifies a future and a hope.

Suggested further reading

MARGARET ATWOOD, *The Handmaid's Tale* (London: Virago, 1987).

ADRIANA CAVARERO, *In Spite of Plato* (London: Polity, 1995).

GRACE M. JANTZEN, *Becoming Divine: Towards a Feminist Philosophy of Religion* (Manchester: Manchester University Press, 1998).

NOTES

CHAPTER 1

1. A. Bredius and H. Gerson, *Rembrandt: The Complete Edition of the Paintings* (London: Phaidon, 1971), nos 620–27.

2. H. S. Chamberlain, *Die Grundlagen des 19. Jahrhunderts* (Munich: Bruckmann, 1899).

3. See S. Krauss, *Das Leben Jesu nach jüdischen Quellen* (Berlin, 1902).

4. See Morton Smith, *Jesus the Magician* (London: Gollancz, 1978), pp. 45–67.

5. Geiger's views on Christianity are most fully worked out in his *Judenthum und seine Geschichte* 3 vols (Breslau: Skutsch, 1865–71).

6. S. Heschel, *Abraham Geiger and the Jewish Jesus* (Chicago: University of Chicago Press, 1998).

7. Joseph Klausner, *Jesus of Nazareth: His Life, Times and Teaching,* translated from the original Hebrew by Herbert Danby (London: Allen & Unwin: 1925).

8. Klausner, *Jesus of Nazareth,* pp. 229–38.

9. Klausner, *Jesus of Nazareth,* p. 232.

10. E. P. Sanders, *Jesus and Judaism* (London: SCM Press, 1985).

11. Klausner, *Jesus of Nazareth,* p. 413.

12. Klausner, *Jesus of Nazareth,* pp. 371–2.

13. Klausner, *Jesus of Nazareth,* p. 414.

14. Klausner, *Jesus of Nazareth,* p. 371.

15. Susannah Heschel suggests that the message of Klausner's *Jesus of Nazareth* is 'to reject Jewish nationhood is to end up like Jesus, as a Christian' (*Abraham Geiger and the Jewish Jesus,* p. 236).

16. G. Vermes, *Jesus the Jew* (London: Collins, 1973; 5th impression with new Preface, London: SCM Press, 1994); *Jesus and the World of Judaism* (SCM Press: London, 1983); *The Religion of Jesus the Jew* (London: SCM Press, 1993); *The Changing Faces of Jesus* (London: Allen Lane, The Penguin Press, 2000).

17. Vermes, *Jesus the Jew*, p. 20.

18. Vermes, *Jesus the Jew*, p. 223.

19. Vermes, *Jesus the Jew*, p. 224.

20. Vermes, *Jesus the Jew*, p. 10. The quotation from Buber may be found in 'Christus, Chassidismus, Gnosis', *Werke*, vol. III (Munich: Kösel and Heidelberg: Lambert Schneider, 1963), p. 937. The claim is reinforced by a further quotation from Buber which opens the Postscript to *Jesus the Jew* (p. 223): 'I am more than ever certain that a great place belongs to (Jesus) in Israel's history of faith . . . There is something in Israel's history of faith which is only to be understood from Israel . . .' (Buber, *Two Types of Faith* [New York: Harper Torchbooks, 1961], p. 13).

21. G. Vermes, *Providential Accidents* (London: SCM Press, 1998).

CHAPTER 2

1. Joseph Ernest Renan, *Histoire du peuple d'Israël* (Paris: Calman, 1891), 5.70.

2. References to the Dead Sea Scrolls are commonly given in one of two ways: by cave number (1 = Cave 1, discovered in 1947; 4 = Cave 4, discovered in 1952), geographical location (Q = Qumran; Mas = Masada), and number (521 = Messianic Apocalypse) or letter (H = *Hodayot* or Thanksgiving Hymns Scroll), or by cave number and place followed by the commonly accepted name of the composition contained in the manuscript. 4Q521 is commonly known as the Messianic Apocalypse and is available in English in Geza Vermes, *The Complete Dead Sea Scrolls in English* (5th edn; London: Penguin Books, 1997), pp. 391–2.

3. All biblical translations are taken from the *New Revised Standard Version* unless otherwise stated.

4. John J. Collins ('The Works of the Messiah', *Dead Sea Discoveries* 1 [1994], p. 107) comments on this parallel that 'It is quite possible that the author of the Sayings source knew 4Q521; at the least he drew on a common tradition'.

5. 4Q246 has been published in its official edition in George Brooke et al. (eds) *Qumran Cave 4.XVII: Parabiblical Texts, Part 3* (Discoveries in the Judaean Desert 22; Oxford: Clarendon Press, 1996), pp. 165–84. It is readily available in English in Geza Vermes, *The Complete Dead Sea Scrolls in English*, pp. 576–7.

6. A summary of the various views can be found in John J. Collins, *The Sceptre and the Star: The Messiahs of the Dead Sea Scrolls and Other Ancient Literature* (New York: Doubleday, 1995), pp. 154–72.

7. This effective translation is by Michael O. Wise, *The First Messiah: Investigating the Savior Before Christ* (San Francisco: HarperSanFrancisco, 1999), p. 105.

8. An idea first put forward by William H. Brownlee, 'Messianic Motifs of Qumran and the New Testament', *New Testament Studies* 3 (1956–7), pp. 12–30.

9. This is the translation of Florentino García Martínez, *The Dead Sea Scrolls Translated* (2nd edn; Leiden: Brill, 1996), p. 127.

10. Vermes, *The Complete Dead Sea Scrolls in English*, p. 159.

11. Michael Wise's two alternative translations are in Michael Wise, Martin Abegg and Edward Cook, *The Dead Sea Scrolls: A New Translation* (New York: HarperCollins, 1996), p. 147. The alternative proposal is by Emile Puech, 'Préséance sacerdotale et Messie-Roi dans la Règle de la Congrégation (1QSa ii 11–22)', *Revue de Qumrân* 16 (1994), pp. 351–66.

12. Lawrence H. Schiffman, *The Eschatological Community of the Dead Sea Scrolls* (Atlanta: Scholars Press, 1989), p. 54, n. 6.

13. The official edition of the manuscript was produced by Dominique Barthélemy in Dominique Barthélemy and Josef T. Milik (eds), *Qumran Cave I* (Discoveries in the Judaean Desert of Jordan 1; Oxford: Clarendon Press, 1955), p. 117. The recent edition by Florentino García Martínez is in Florentino García Martínez and Eibert J. C. Tigchelaar, *The Dead Sea Scrolls Study Edition*, Vol. 1 *1Q1–4Q273* (Leiden: Brill, 1997), p. 102.

14. This is the translation in the principal edition of the manuscript by Emanuel Tov and Sidnie White in Harold Attridge *et al.* (eds), *Qumran Cave 4. VIII: Parabiblical Texts, Part I* (Discoveries in the Judaean Desert 13; Oxford: Clarendon Press, 1994), p. 270.

15. This fragmentary song has not been commented upon in any great detail, but see George J. Brooke, 'Power to the Powerless: A Long-Lost Song of Miriam', *Biblical Archaeology Review* 20/3 (May–June 1994), pp. 62–5.

16. For some general comments on how the Benedictus (Luke 2.68–79) may similarly reflect the language of some of the Dead Sea Scrolls, see Raymond E. Brown, *A Coming Christ in Advent: Essays on the Gospel Narratives Preparing for the Birth of Jesus (Matthew 1 and Luke 1)* (Collegeville: The Liturgical Press, 1988), p. 51.

CHAPTER 3

1. On the ideas of implied readers see Wolfgang Iser, *The Implied Reader: Patterns of Communication in Prose Fiction from Bunyan to Beckett* (Baltimore: Johns Hopkins University Press, 1974).

2. For a critical account of key or root symbols and the way they organise cultural meanings, see James W. Fernandez (ed.), *Beyond Metaphor: The Theory of Tropes in Anthropology* (Stanford: Stanford University Press, 1991).

3. Daniel Boyarin, *Carnal Israel: Reading Sex in Talmudic Culture* (Berkeley: University of California Press, 1993), p. 7.

4. Quoted in Boyarin, *Carnal Israel*, p. 8.

5. See Jonathan Sawday, *The Body Emblazoned: Dissection and the Human Body in Renaissance Culture* (London: Routledge, 1995).

6. See Dale Martin, *The Corinthian Body* (New Haven: Yale University Press, 1995).

7. John O' Malley, *Praise and Blame in Renaissance Rome: Rhetoric, Doctrine and Reform in the Sacred Orators of the Papal Court, c.1450–1521* (Durham: Duke University Press 1979); see also Leo Steinberg *The Sexuality of Christ in Renaissance Art and in Modern Oblivion* (Chicago: University of Chicago Press, 1996).

8. Quoted in Steinberg, *The Sexuality of Christ*, p. 63.

9. Elliot Wolfson, *Circle in the Square: Studies in the Use of Gender in Kabbalistic Symbolism* (Albany: State University of New York Press, 1995), p. 30.

10. Wolfson, *Circle in the Square*, p. 42.

11. Wolfson, *Circle in the Square*, p. 45.

CHAPTER 4

1. A classic overview of this region of Paul's theology is offered by L. Cerfaux, *Christ in the Theology of St Paul* (trans. G. Webb; New York: Herder & Herder, 1959), pp. 161–92.

2. All biblical quotations are from the *NRSV*, unless otherwise noted.

3. Cf. *NASB* text and margin; note also 'seed' (of Abraham), Galatians 3.16.

4. D. Wenham, *Paul: Follower of Jesus or Founder of Christianity?* (Grand Rapids: Eerdmans, 1995), pp. 338–43; see also D. Wenham, 'The Story of Jesus Known to Paul', in J. B. Green and M. Turner (eds), *Jesus of Nazareth: Lord and Christ: Essays on the Historical Jesus and New Testament Christology* (Grand Rapids: Eerdmans; Carlisle: Paternoster, 1994), pp. 298–301. This question of Paul's knowledge of narrative tradition is distinct from that of the *sayings* of Jesus, knowledge of which on Paul's part Wenham gives a notably high estimate.

5. Wenham, it should be added, is not unaware of these difficulties.

6. Wenham, *Paul*, p. 339.

7. Wenham, *Paul*, pp. 339–40.

8. Wenham, *Paul*, p. 340.

9. I leave to one side 'born under law' in Galatians 4.4 as indicating circumcision and Temple ritual in connection with childbirth (linked by Wenham to Luke 2.22–24); the link appears somewhat strained, and at any rate this too is very general. Furthermore, the significance of 'born under law' is subject to interpretative debate: see J. L. Martyn, *Galatians* (Anchor Bible 33A; New York: Doubleday, 1997), p. 390.

10. Wenham, *Paul*, p. 339.

11. Wenham, *Paul*, pp. 340–1, 343.

12. Wenham, *Paul*, pp. 341–3; 'Story', pp. 298–300 (more emphasis is placed in this latter work on the question of the virgin birth in Paul); Wenham draws here on C. E. B. Cranfield, 'Some Reflections on the Subject of the Virgin Birth', *Scottish Journal of Theology* 41 (1988), pp. 177–89, reprint in *On Romans and Other New Testament Essays* (Edinburgh: T&T Clark, 1998), pp. 151–65 (see p. 153); cf. *The Epistle to the Romans*, Vol. I (ICC; Edinburgh: T&T Clark, 1975), p. 59; Cranfield finds a hint of the virgin birth in Mark as well, reading beneath the reference to Jesus as the 'son of Mary' (Mark 6.3): see 'Some Reflections', pp. 153–4, and cf. Wenham, *Paul*, p. 338 n. 3. Another christological question sometimes taken up in connection with Paul's verb usage in the texts in question is that of 'pre-existence'; but this is a separate matter, not touched on here.

13. Wenham, *Paul*, pp. 342–3. For the former argument, Wenham cites J. D. G. Dunn, *Romans* (Word Biblical Commentary 38A; Dallas: Word, 1988), p. 12, and J. D. G. Dunn, *The Epistle to the Galatians* (Black's New Testament Commentary; London: A&C Black, 1993), p. 215; for the latter, he cites F. F. Bruce, *The Epistle to the Galatians: A Commentary on the Greek Text* (New International Greek Testament Commentary; Grand Rapids: Eerdmans, 1982), p. 195. See also H. D. Betz, *Galatians: A Commentary on Paul's Letter to the Churches in Galatia* (Hermeneia; Philadelphia: Fortress, 1979), pp. 207–8 and nn. 52, 55; R. N. Longenecker, *Galatians* (Word Biblical Commentary, 41; Dallas: Word, 1990), p. 171; J. A. Fitzmyer, *Romans* (Anchor Bible 33; New York: Doubleday, 1993), p. 234.

14. Here I employ the terms of D. A. Cruse, *Lexical Semantics* (Cambridge Textbooks in Linguistics; Cambridge: Cambridge University Press, 1986), pp. 49–83; Cruse's approach there is updated in his *Meaning in Language: An Introduction to Semantics and Pragmatics* (Oxford Linguistics; Oxford: Oxford University Press, 2000), pp. 105–24; my observations on the verbs in question are in keeping with the treatment in J. P. Louw and E. A. Nida

(eds), *Greek–English Lexicon of the New Testament Based on Semantic Domains* (2nd edn; New York: United Bible Societies, 1988, 1989), an important starting point for semantic analysis.

15. Thus, Wenham's statistical arguments from wider usage (*Paul,* pp. 341–2; 'Story', p. 299) might well backfire; or, at least, they are neutralised by contextual factors, and by the fact that Paul himself hardly uses the terms in question (in the relevant sense) enough to establish a pattern. As to Wenham's comparison with *gennaō* in Galatians 4.23, 29, the latter might also be influenced by contextual factors (see Martyn, *Galatians,* pp. 434, 451–4).

16. Wenham, 'Story', p. 300. On Matthew in relation to the question here, see R. E. Brown, *The Birth of the Messiah: A Commentary on the Infancy Narratives in the Gospels of Matthew and Luke* (2nd edn; New York: Doubleday, 1993), pp. 61–2, 130, 518–19; cf. Wenham, *Paul,* p. 343 n. 19.

17. F. J. Matera's succinct comment on Galatians 4.4 gets the balance right: Paul's choice of words 'neither implies nor denies the virgin birth'; *Galatians* (Sacra Pagina, 9; Collegeville: Liturgical Press, 1992), p. 150.

18. On this, see S. G. Wilson, 'From Jesus to Paul: The Contours and Consequences of a Debate', in P. Richardson and J. C. Hurd (eds), *From Jesus to Paul: Studies in Honour of Francis Wright Beare* (Waterloo, Ontario: Wilfrid Laurier University Press, 1984), pp. 1–21.

19. W. Wrede, *Paul* (trans. E. Lummis; London: Philip Green, 1907), pp. 179, 180.

20. There are two aspects to Wenham's book, one in which he seeks to trace out theological similarities between Jesus and Paul, the other in which he argues for Paul's extensive dependence on Jesus-tradition. I would concur with M. D. Hooker's verdict: 'Although Wenham's attempts to prove direct dependence on Jesus' teaching are largely unpersuasive, his book succeeds in underlining the continuity between the thought of Jesus and Paul'; Review of Wenham, *Paul,* in *Journal of Biblical Literature* 115 (1996), pp. 756–8 (758). This verdict is in keeping with V. P. Furnish's conclusion that 'the Jesus–Paul debate has not ever been significantly advanced, nor will a solution to the Jesus–Paul problem ever be finally achieved, by locating parallel passages in Paul and the Gospels'; V. P. Furnish, 'The Jesus–Paul Debate: From Baur to Bultmann', in A. J. M. Wedderburn (ed.), *Paul and Jesus: Collected Essays* (JSNTSup 37; Sheffield: Sheffield Academic Press, 1989), pp. 17–50 (44).

21. On this terminology of 'minimalist' versus 'maximalist', see, e.g. S. Kim, 'Jesus, Sayings of', in G. F. Hawthorne and R. P. Martin (eds), *Dictionary*

of Paul and His Letters (Downers Grove: InterVarsity Press, 1993), pp. 474–92.

22. Note Wenham's characterisation of what is at stake in this debate: 'the legitimacy of Pauline and traditional Christianity' (*Paul*, p. 8).

23. This point is put well by J. M. G. Barclay, 'Jesus and Paul', in *Dictionary of Paul and His Letters*, pp. 492–503 (see p. 499), an excellent overview of the debate.

24. I am adapting an axiom attributed by J. P. Meier to J. Neusner ('What you cannot show, you do not know'); see J. P. Meier, 'Dividing Lines in Jesus Research Today: Through Dialectical Negation to a Positive Sketch', in J. D. Kingsbury (ed.), *Gospel Interpretation: Narrative-Critical and Social-Scientific Approaches* (Harrisburg: Trinity Press International, 1997), pp. 253–72 (256). One might reasonably ask whether this 'historical' stance is best suited to a 'faith' context or perspective – but then wasn't our question (Paul and the birth of Jesus) a *historical* one?

25. V. A. Harvey, *A Handbook of Theological Terms* (New York: Touchstone, 1997 [1964]), p. 248.

26. J. W. McClendon, Jr, *Doctrine: Systematic Theology II* (Nashville: Abingdon, 1994), p. 270 (emphasis removed).

27. Works typically associated with a 'narrative reading' of Paul include R. B. Hays, *The Faith of Jesus Christ: An Investigation of the Narrative Substructure of Galatians 3.1–4.11* (SBLDS 56, Chico: Scholars Press, 1983); S. E. Fowl, *The Story of Christ in the Ethics of Paul: An Analysis of the Function of the Hymnic Material in the Pauline Corpus* (JSNTSup 36; Sheffield: Sheffield Academic Press, 1990); N. T. Wright, *The Climax of the Covenant: Christ and the Law in Pauline Theology* (Edinburgh: T&T Clark, 1991); and B. Witherington III, *Paul's Narrative Thought World: The Tapestry of Tragedy and Triumph* (Louisville: Westminster/John Knox Press, 1994).

28. Wrede, *Paul*, p. 85.

29. Wrede, *Paul*, pp. 88–9.

30. Wrede, *Paul*, p. 148.

31. Wrede, *Paul*, p. 165.

32. Wrede, *Paul*, pp. 178–9 (emphasis removed).

33. It is interesting to compare L. T. Johnson's comments on the 'mythic' and the 'human' Jesus in Paul: *Living Jesus: Learning the Heart of the Gospel* (New York: HarperSanFrancisco, 1999), pp. 99–115.

34. See Galatians 4.1–7; Romans 8.12–17, 23; on this theme, see J. M. Scott, 'Adoption, Sonship', in *Dictionary of Paul and His Letters*, pp. 15–18.

35. At the Symposium, I noted with interest E. Graham's treatment of the celebration of the Christmas story (see below pp. 89–98).

36. Note, again, the work of Hays *et al.* As to contemporary theological interests and the question of the virgin birth, I noted with interest at the Symposium G. Brooke's question of metaphorical versus literal interpretation, A. Peacocke's emphasis on the theological importance of the full humanity of Jesus, and G. Jantzen's characterisation of recent theological emphases (see chapters 2, 5 and 9 in this volume).

CHAPTER 5

1. Raymond E. Brown, *The Virginal Conception and Bodily Resurrection of Jesus* (New York: Paulist Press, 1973), p. 42.

2. Brown, *The Virginal Conception and Bodily Resurrection of Jesus*, p. 42, n. 56, citing Ratzinger's *Introduction to Christianity* (New York: Herder & Herder, 1969), p. 208.

3. Michael J. Langford, *Providence* (London: SCM Press, 1981), pp. 18–19.

4. Raymond E. Brown, *The Birth of the Messiah* (London: Geoffrey Chapman, and Garden City, New York: Doubleday, 1977), p. 527, emphasis in text.

5. Brown, *The Birth of the Messiah*, p. 527, n. 26a.

6. John Macquarrie, *Jesus Christ in Modern Thought* (London: SCM Press, 1990), pp. 392–3.

7. C. J. Cadoux, *The Life of Jesus* (Harmondsworth: Penguin Books, 1948), p. 30.

8. Derek Stanseby, 'Notes on Biology and Salvation', *The Annual Review of St George's House, Windsor* (1990), p. 28; see also his article on the 'Nature of Jesus and his genes', *The Times*, 12 December 1987, for a similar statement.

9. Stanseby, 'Notes on Biology and Salvation', p. 28.

10. Macquarrie, *Jesus Christ in Modern Thought*, p. 393.

11. Gregory of Nazianzus, Ep. 101, *Nicene and Post-Nicene Fathers* (Parker, 1894), quoted in H. Bettenson, *Documents of the Christian Church* (London: Oxford University Press, 1943, reprinted 1956), p. 64.

12. 'Docetism (from Greek *dokeo* – I seem) refers to the doctrine that the manhood of Christ was apparent not real, that as in some Greek myths, a divine being was dressed up as a man in order to communicate revelations, but was not really involved in the human state and withdrew before the passion': Frances Young, 'Docetism', in *A New Dictionary of Christian Theology* (eds A. Richardson and J. Bowden; London: SCM Press, 1983), p. 160. The adjective 'docetic' is widely used to denote doctrines or views which tend in this direction and which imply that the humanity of Jesus was not real.

13. Ironically, according to Raymond Brown, the credal statement 'born of the virgin Mary' was intended, by shifting the emphasis to birth, to signal 'that *part* of the interest was now on the reality of Jesus' humanity against a docetic heresy: the proof of his humanity is that we know the agents of his birth (Mary) and death (Pontius Pilate)' (*A New Dictionary of Christian Theology*, p. 598). Today, in the light of biology – and of historical studies – it has an opposite, docetic, tendency.

CHAPTER 6

1. A. Schopenhauer, 'On Women', in *Essays and Aphorisms* (trans. R. J. Hollingdale; London: Penguin Books, 1970), p. 86.

2. Schopenhauer, 'On Women', pp. 86–7.

3. Cf. S. de Beauvoir, *The Second Sex* (trans. H. M. Parshley; London: Pan Books, 1988), p. 230.

4. F. Nietzsche, *Beyond Good and Evil: Prelude to a Philosophy of the Future* (trans. R. J. Hollingdale; London: Penguin Books, 1990), p. 163.

5. Nietzsche, *Beyond Good and Evil*, p. 164.

6. Cf. M. Y. MacDonald, *Early Christian Women and Pagan Opinion: The Power of the Hysterical Woman* (Cambridge: Cambridge University Press, 1996), pp. 154–65.

7. De Beauvoir, *The Second Sex*, pp. 313–17.

8. G. R. Craig, *Germany 1866–1945* (Oxford: Oxford University Press, 1981), pp. 207–13.

9. W. Carr, *A History of Germany 1815–1945* (London: Edward Arnold, 1969), p. 28.

10. Craig, *Germany 1866–1945*, p. 207.

11. Craig, *Germany 1866–1945*, p. 207.

12. Craig, *Germany 1866–1945*, p. 207; see also J. M. Thompson, *The French Revolution* (2nd edn with revised bibliography; Oxford: Blackwell, 1985), pp. 93–5.

13. J. Pelikan, *Mary through the Centuries: Her Place in the History of Culture* (New Haven and London: Yale University Press, 1996), p. 219.

14. See, e.g. C. F. D. Moule, 'Excursis II: Luke and the Pastoral Epistles', in *The Birth of the New Testament* (2nd edn; London: A&C Black, 1966), pp. 220–1.

15. E. Haenchen, *The Acts of the Apostles: A Commentary* (trans. B. Noble and G. Shinn; Oxford: Blackwell, 1971), p. 116.

16. E. Haenchen, *The Acts of the Apostles*, p. 116.

17. Cf. T. K. Seim, *The Double Message: Patterns of Gender in Luke–Acts* (Edinburgh: T&T Clark, 1994), pp. 194–8, 247–8, 258–9.

18. Seim, *The Double Message*, p. 180.

19. For detailed support of this reading of 1 Timothy 2.15, see S. E. Porter, 'What Does It Mean to be "Saved by Childbirth" (1 Tim. 2.15)?', *Journal for the Study of the New Testament* 49 (1993), pp. 87–102.

20. Cf. MacDonald, *Early Christian Women*, pp. 157–65.

21. Cf. Seim, *The Double Message*, pp. 247–8.

22. For further discussion with similar conclusions, see J. B. Green, *The Gospel of Luke* (New International Commentary on the New Testament; Grand Rapids and Cambridge: William B. Eerdmans, 1997), pp. 85–6.

23. Cf. Seim, *The Double Message*, pp. 175–8.

24. See, e.g. R. Laurentin, *Structure et Théologie de Luc I–II* (Etudes Bibliques; Paris: Gabalda, 1957), pp. 26–33.

25. See 1 Corinthians 1.12–17; 3.4–6, 21–23; 4.6; 16.12.

26. For two very different, but ultimately reconcilable, discussions of Apollos which taken together lend weighty support to this suggestion, see S. Pétrement, *A Separate God: The Christian Origins of Gnosticism* (trans. C. Harrison; San Francisco: Harper & Row, 1990), pp. 248–64, 280–8, 483; and B. W. Winter, *Philo and Paul among the Sophists* (Society for New Testament Studies Monograph Series; Cambridge: Cambridge University Press, 1997), pp. 174–7, 200, 241.

CHAPTER 7

1. See, for example, G. Finaldi and others, *The Image of Christ: The Catalogue of the Exhibition 'Seeing Salvation'* (London: National Gallery Company, distributed by Yale University Press, 2000); the exhibition 'Seeing Salvation' was held at the National Gallery, London, 26 February–7 May 2000, to mark the end of the second millennium since the birth of Jesus.

2. See Grace Davie, *Religion in Britain since 1945: Believing Without Belonging* (Oxford: Blackwell, 1994).

3. Adapted from John Wolffe, 'The Religions of the Silent Majority', in G. Parsons (ed.), *The Growth of Religious Diversity: Britain from 1945* (London: Routledge, 1993), pp. 305–46, although the term 'vernacular' religion, denoting that of common speech, is my own addition.

4. However orchestrated or open to suggestion they may have been by media coverage.

5. James A. Beckford, 'Religion, Modernity and Post-modernity', in Bryan Wilson (ed.), *Religion: Contemporary Issues: The All Souls Seminar in the Sociology of Religion* (London: Bellew, 1992), pp. 11–23.

6. William Paden, *Religious Worlds* (Boston: Beacon Press, 2nd edn, 1994).

7. Marie McCarthy, 'Spirituality in a Postmodern Era', in S. Pattison and J. W. Woodward (eds), *The Blackwell Reader in Pastoral and Practical Theology* (Oxford: Blackwell, 2000), pp. 192–206.

8. As in the use of the internet and electronic mail to transcend distances of space and time.

9. Stephen Kepnes, 'Telling and Retelling; the Use of Narrative in Psychoanalysis and Religion', *Concilium* 156 (1988), pp. 27–33.

10. Gerard Loughlin, *Telling God's Story: Bible, Church and Narrative Theology* (Cambridge: Cambridge University Press, 1996), p. 119.

11. George Stroup, *The Promise of Narrative Theology* (London: SCM Press, 1984), p. 124.

12. Loughlin, *Telling God's Story*, pp. 113–14.

13. Heather Walton, 'True Vine', in H. Walton and S. Durber (eds), *Silence in Heaven* (London: SCM Press, 1994), pp. 169–72.

CHAPTER 8

1. Lucian of Samosata, *Dialogues of the Dead* 11 (16), present author's translation; but see also M. D. Macleod, ed. and trans, *Lucian* VII (Loeb Classical Library; London: Harvard University Press, 1961), pp. 402–5. For the importance of Cynic philosophers for early Christians, see F. G. Downing, *Cynics and Christian Origins* (Edinburgh: T&T Clark, 1992), esp. ch. 7, pp. 179–202.

2. Justin Martyr, *First Apology* ('Answer to Critics'), 21; compare Justin's *Dialogue with Trypho, a Jew*, 66.

3. Grace Jantzen, *Becoming Divine: Towards a Feminist Philosophy of Religion* (Manchester: Manchester University Press, 1998); and in this volume pp. 111–21.

4. For the importance of avoiding self-projection, see for instance David Cheetham, 'Postmodern Freedom and Religion', *Theology* CIII 811 (2000), pp. 29–36.

5. This distinction may be made and discussed elsewhere, but I have not met it in this form. I advanced it in F. Gerald Downing, *Doing Theology Thoughtfully . . . The Theologians' Craft* (Manchester: Downing, 1974). Garrett Green, *Imagining God* (San Francisco: Harper & Row, 1989), makes

a similar point by contrasting 'imagining as' with 'imagining as if', especially pp. 134–41. I prefer my own formulation.

6. Dennis Potter, *Hide and Seek* (London: André Deutsch, 1973).

7. 'Ontological' means concerned with 'being', with what 'is' (from part of the Greek verb 'to be'), and Anselm in the twelfth century argued 'Something than which a greater cannot be conceived undoubtedly both stands in relation to the understanding and exists in reality' (for if it did not exist in reality it would be less than the greatest imaginable). The argument fails to convince as it stands. It rightly emphasises that the God we imagine can only be imagined as real, but does not show that imagining him so is inescapable.

8. See, e.g. G. A. Lindbeck, *The Nature of Doctrine: Religion and Theology in a Postliberal Age* (London: SPCK, 1984), and D. Z. Phillips, *Faith After Foundationalism* (London: Routledge, 1988).

9. F. Gerald Downing, *A Man for Us and a God for Us* (London: Epworth, 1968). For essays in incarnational theology to which this chapter seeks to relate: B. Hebblethwaite, *The Incarnation* (Cambridge: Cambridge University Press, 1987); A. Thatcher, *Truly a Person, Truly God* (London: SPCK, 1990); R. Sturch, *The Word and the Christ* (Oxford: Clarendon Press, 1991); and for an overview, J. Macquarrie, *Christology Revisited* (London: SCM Press, 1998).

10. 'Theotokos' is usually translated 'Mother of God,' 'Mater Dei'; but '-tokos' can be used of male begetter or of female conceiver in ancient Greek. As 'parent to God incarnate' it could now apply as well to Joseph as to Mary as we understand human genetics.

CHAPTER 9

1. Margaret Atwood, *The Handmaid's Tale* (London: Virago, 1987).

2. P. D. James, *The Children of Men* (London: Penguin Books, 1992).

3. I am indebted to the work of Hannah Arendt, read against the grain. For a fuller discussion of her work and of these characteristics, see my *Becoming Divine: Towards a Feminist Philosophy of Religion* (Manchester: Manchester University Press, 1998), chapter 6.

4. Joanna Vecchiarelli Scott and Judith Chelius Stark (eds), *Love and Saint Augustine* (Chicago: University of Chicago Press, 1996), p. 147; from *City of God* xii.20: '*Initium ut esset, creatus est homo, ante quem nemo fuit.*'

5. Hannah Arendt, *Between Past and Future* (Harmondsworth: Penguin Books, 1977), p. 167; cf. my *Becoming Divine*, p. 145.

INDEX OF REFERENCES

INDEX OF NAMES

Figures in **bold** type refer to the essays in this book